**Also by Joe Arrigo**

*The Secret Factor for Uncommon Sales Success*

*Universal Mysteries*

*Exceptional Italian Dishes from the Old Neighborhood*

*Colorful and Creative Similes to Dress Up, Add Punch and Make Your Writing Dance*

*Insights Into Health and Well Being*

*Enthusiasm IS the Enemy: Get Fit Stay Fit*

*Profound Quotations to Guide and Renovate Your Life*

# Table of Contents

## Introduction

## Feelings and Logic.................................. 1
Rephrase the Content and Reflect the Feeling
Skilled Listening
Emotion as Decider
The Need to Feel Important
The Feeling that Saved the World

## Strategies of Emotional Connection ....... 28
Setting the Stage
Techniques
Assertiveness
Surrendering Our People Skills through Modern Technology

## Ego and Competence............................ 79
The Man in the Ape Suit
Taming the Ego: Enhancing Competence

## Non-Adversarial Negotiation: Real or Oxymoron?............................................. 104
Utilizing Emotions Toward Agreement

The Power of Cooperation ........................ 120
  Science and Religion
  Mutualism and Altruism
  Genuine Progress Indicator
  Tribalism
  Our Environment
  Belief Systems
  In Conclusion

Bibliography ............................................. 165

Acknowledgements .................................. 172

# Introduction

Influencing people is to enlist their cooperation. Cooperation literally means "working together," from the Latin "co", together; and "operare", to work. The elements that are necessary to engage cooperation are; it requires excellent communication between all parties, the establishment of a shared understanding of the goals desired, in most cases a mutual benefit of all participants, the effort of each to reach and maintain those goals, and the awareness of others' feelings. Cooperation from others is what we all rely on to live our lives to the fullest; the more cooperation we can get, the happier we can be. Unless you're a cave dweller, we need each other. Working together, great things happen.

Fundamentally, cooperation is based on a win/win mentality: it emphasizes interdependence rather than independence and competition, where interdependence should not be confused with dependence, the former comes from a place of strength, and needs independent participants for it to work, and dependence comes from a place of weakness where it could never forge an interdependent relationship.

A win/win way of doing things may seem idealistic to many, where they look out and perhaps see a tough selfish world, yet ironically, that's precisely what can bring us together because mutual benefit does, in fact, speak to the selfish side as well as the generous side of ourselves. What part of *win* couldn't any of us understand? What part of it isn't in our best interest? Win/lose comes from a place of inflated ego, playing the zero-sum game of I cannot feel a win unless you lose, uninterested in solving problems; it's only about a power struggle, and of being *right*. Ego reveres competition; facts become threatening and ignored, and is the antithesis of cooperation, where it attempts to inflate itself further.

It's understandable, because so much of society is based on competition—sports, the Olympics, business, politics, entertainment—all, a win/lose scenario. Yet ironically, even in those intense arenas, cooperation is at the core of success; the individual teams practice cooperation to be their best, individual companies are as successful as their internal cooperation, and politics rely heavily on the cooperative effort of their constituency to deliver victory.

Cooperation and win/win are reliant upon one of the greatest evolutionary marvels between species—communication. From bacteria, that communicate chemically, to ants that have a communication system of touch and pheromones so sophisticated it acts as one organism, to many oceanic animals that communicate through sound. We homo sapiens, through the phenomenal invention of words and language, seem to have the most elaborate communication system in the history of life; not only could we communicate through sound, we could also communicate silently through the next phenomenal invention of the written word. Language accelerated cooperation, and thereby accelerated our evolution, a quantum leap in exchanging thoughts, leading to man's dominion of planet Earth. Using communication in the quest of influencing people is what this book is about.

In reading this book, it is my sincere hope you come away with a renewed sense of how valuable cooperation can be, and an excitement for the powerful tools and concepts presented here in developing effective skills to influence others.

# Feelings and Logic

*Listen to what I mean, not what I say.*
—Anonymous

Feelings are at the heart of who we are, and influencing others. We are not cold, automaton-like thinking machines. Without our consent, our feelings are activated automatically, and when they are, the person feeling them, especially with the instantaneous reflex-action of fear which functions for our benefit as a survival mechanism, does not question them. Charles Darwin once tested this reaction to determine whether it was controllable,

> I put my face close to the thick glass-plate in front of a puff-adder in the Zoological Gardens, with the firm determination of not starting back if the snake struck at me; but, as soon as the blow was struck, my resolution went for nothing, and I jumped a yard or two backwards with astonishing rapidity. My will and reason were powerless against the imagination of a danger which had never been experienced.[1]

Our feelings are trusted as any other facet of our perception is trusted, whether they are insightful, keenly perceptive, rational, irrational or biased. We could, of course, exercise control over biases, provided we were aware of them, however, many times they percolate from our unconscious, making it quite challenging in controlling them. That hardly makes our emotions undesirable. Can any of us imagine a life without them? It's what we live for, in the pursuit of joy, love, pleasure, and fulfillment. We pursue feeling good. Life would hardly be worth living without them.

This is the vital role our feelings play in the enjoyment of life, therefore, developing a high appreciation for human feelings should help us make allowances for other people when they display them, even when they may be somewhat irritating to us. In many ways it will be much to our advantage to do so, as we will cover. One distinction about feelings that is crucial to be recognized here is that emotions are only a part of feelings, and that many unconscious nudges that bubble-up are a part of our intellect as well, therefore, feelings have their own brand of intelligence.

For those who tend to be analytical and logical, they are inclined to converse with people on that basis alone, and where they can go wrong is to take each and everything a person has to say, hold it up, and examine it under the cold light of logic, seemingly blind to the fact that we are all creatures of feelings and emotions. A phrase I heard once sums it up, "Pistol-whipped with common sense." When we do this`, we subtly, and many times not so subtly, alienate the person we're speaking to, because we won't allow that human being any latitude in his or her expression.

In effect, it is wholly illogical to dialogue with another person in that manner, to say nothing of unskillful, especially if we're attempting to enlist his or her cooperation. This is true in business as well as on a personal level—all areas of life. People who function in the mostly logical, rational, left-brain realm of thinking are utilizing only half of their problem solving capacity. That kind of thinking is limited because it's more of a binary system, where many roadblocks will thwart progress. The dominant left-brain thinkers can learn to relax that part of themselves and with a little practice, incorporate their right brain into the process where creative options are the perfect compliment to their strong rational thought.

Because our formal education emphasizes left-brain development, the right brain becomes somewhat dormant, and needs to be reawakened. The left-brain may only see your way and the "wrong" way, where using both sides can come to realize a *third alternative*. If we can learn to value the differences in our views, to entertain the possibility that we're both correct, that everything doesn't have to be in opposition or binary, and that there's usually a third possibility when we creatively explore options, we then can move beyond many limitations.

Insisting on holding their feet to the fire using logic alone denies people their humanness, and a definite impediment to getting your thinking through to people—it's all about communication—the single most important factor in human harmony that affects every level of our relationships. We need to keep in mind that each of us comes from the perspective of our own individual logic, and, it may seem completely illogical to the other person. We need also to be cognizant of, and respectful of the fact, that because people exhibit their feelings, doesn't mean their personas are flawed.

Many whopper errors have resulted by means of reason, and much wisdom has been derived from the heart. There are few of us who haven't sought the advice of others we knew well who weren't as educated or knowledgeable or worldly as ourselves, yet they possessed a certain aura of judgment based on their feelings and insight we valued; when they spoke, we listened. Sometimes pure logic clouds and narrows the mind, where we tend to lose our innate human perception, denouncing our inner voice, and go astray revering rationale; outsmarting ourselves. Columbo and Monk would prove it every week.

Have you ever witnessed a debate where one side successfully influenced the other side to change its mind? Very doubtful—because debate is not about communication, it's about winning, and the basis for winning involves the ego. A clever debater can deliberately misrepresent an opponent's words to mean something other than what that person intended. It's purely a tactic to win; even humiliate. No doubt it creates animosity where the drive to win at all costs is intensified, promoting an atmosphere that's far removed from true communication, much like most political debates. This type of aggressive dialogue is one handed-down to us from the ancient Greeks. In their assemblies, they learned to debate competitively, use logic and theoretical ploys to undermine and discredit their opponents in order to *win*. Defeating the other *was* the object; the name of the game, where changing one's mind or being converted to another view in the name of sincere communication and truth, wasn't even a remote possibility. The late columnist and author, Sydney J. Harris eloquently states,

> Most disputations are fruitless at best because the contestants want to instruct, not to learn; to persuade, not to investigate; to feel justified, not corrected or reproached or convinced of error. And the more heated the controversy, the more both antagonists lose sight of reality, of reason, and of the

common objective to discover where the good resides. What is worse, however, is that arguments tend to polarize; each side becomes more extreme; nothing of value is credited to the other side, not even decent motives, and the disputants turn into bitter enemies. All one has to do is read the history of religious disputation in the seventeenth and eighteenth centuries to see how people pledged to the same God and the same Savior persecuted and slew each other over points of theology no one today even comprehends.

A courtroom trial should be about getting to the truth, yet, it's not being cynical to recognize that a trial is about winning, and winning only, where it's the jury's onerous task to scratch and scrape its way to the truth. So utilizing logic as a lone weapon has the dangerous potential to mutate your bid for cooperation and effectiveness into a contest...the last place you want to be. As the old saying goes, *you won the battle, but you lost the war.*

Many times in the course of conversation the dialogue traverses down the proverbial slippery slope where the thin-skinned fragile ego is engaged, defenses rise, and the would-be constructive conversation descends into a contest of wit, where we listen only for openings in order to twist another's words, as one author states it, "to use them as grist for our own mill." This creates a lose/lose situation. Being aware of this potential danger as an insidious entrapment is the first step to nipping it the bud, thereby navigating the dialogue away from that black hole.


Impatience is a luxury. The reverence for logic and common sense that manifests itself with intolerance for the other person's less than rational view will be costly to what you're trying to achieve. The foremost question to ask yourself when entering into a dialogue with someone you want to positively connect with and influence is this: what can this human being I'm speaking to, *gain* from our conversation? The gain can basically be pleasurable feelings merely by the act of listening attentively, making him or her feel important, sincerely expressing heartfelt admiration for their capabilities and appreciation of their efforts; rendering them far more receptive.

The gain can also be providing the opportunity for that person to vent and process his or her feelings in the course of the conversation, thereby releasing and relieving any anxiety he or she may have pent up, because bringing emotions to the surface reduces tension, and, contributes to a realistic assessment of a problem.

There are two elements to great communication leading to exerting influence. One is the sequence of logic based on the facts, and the other is to satisfy emotional needs. That's not rocket surgery, but easy to lose sight of; as one woman laments to an advice column, "My boyfriend never listens to my feelings."

One must not allow his or her impatience to draw a line of thought into a precipitous logical conclusion, and undermine creating a mood of connectedness with this human being whose eyes you are looking into. Maintain your competence, avoid a verbal contest, and win his or her sense of your sincere involvement.

In the movie, *The Brave One,* with Jodie Foster, she and the man she is completely in love with and adores are attacked by an inner-city gang; her lover is killed, and she, brutalized into unconsciousness. There is a scene where two detectives are questioning her about the crime in a matter-of-fact, no nonsense indifferent manner, and she expresses some exasperation and anger. The detectives remind her with,

"We're on your side,"

Foster says, "Yea, I know, you're the good guys...how come it doesn't feel that way?" The detectives, being insensitive clods, did not earn her cooperation because of the feeling she experienced from their clueless interpersonal incompetence. People need to feel your empathy or there is a disconnect—a lack of trust.

Professor in Medicine at the University of Chicago, Wendy Levinson, did a study looking for the most important reason patients sue their doctors for malpractice, suggesting that that reason was *how* the doctor spoke with the patient, and not medical negligence. They found that the tone of voice of the doctors was more important than what they said. The study comprised 59 family practitioners and 65 surgeons, producing 1,265 audio tapes of routine patient visits, showing that the doctors who were not sued encouraged their patients to express their concerns and opinions, and spent about three minutes longer with them (18.3 minutes vs. 15 minutes).

They also communicated what the patients could expect during the visit, being sure they understood the information, drawing the patients out with questions, and listened well. And, doctors who used humor in their interactions with these patients were also less likely to be sued. "Competence doesn't stop with the technical," said Levinson, and that, "Not enough research has been devoted to the human side of healing." This study is the first empirical research that shows how vital communication and empathy impacts malpractice suits.[2]

Treating people with respect for their humanness, making them feel dignified, looking at them as whole people instead of merely a hunk of meat prevented many patients from suing even though they were harmed. Your acceptance of that (doesn't mean your agreement), will win you enormous influence with them.

Human feelings are not responsive to reason. Meeting those feelings head-on with cold hard reason most likely will exaggerate the emotion, making him or her feel irrational, and probably more emotional. That is not a gain for that person, but a resounding loss, and is not good for either of you. When a person is illogical, it's tempting for most of us to set him or her straight with a mere word or two, thereby winning the battle. It feels good to you, and feels bad to him or her. That's a zero sum game. Win/win is what you're after, but if you give in to the temptation to be right rather than kind and smart, it's not what you get.

It is imperative that you enter into dialogue with sincerity, even though your intent is toward a goal. Entering into conversation with an intent of manipulation can be disastrous because in doing so, you probably will underestimate the perceptiveness of this person—you will get busted; and that person will see through you like a fish-tank. Effectual no-nonsense people are driven to get things done, and done now, therefore, it's difficult for them to use techniques beyond pure reason, and something that has to be worked on. People are not pawns and they must be given the respect they deserve, where patience and sincerity are king and are, in fact, *the* effectual things to execute.

One caveat to keep in mind. Avoid coming across as condescending, where you may insult a person's intelligence. A person who has deep feelings about a particular subject, whether those feelings are illogical or not, does not mean that he or she is stupid. Do not underestimate anyone. People don't have to be articulate to be perceptive, they may not have the verbal skills to eloquently express their views, but most can perceive a gratuitous disingenuous attempt to win them over. Be respectful of their integrity as a fellow human being, always. Feelings are key. The opposite of logical is not emotional; it is irrational. When someone is being emotional when he or she is expressing her or himself, it's a mistake to conclude that he or she is an irrational person, they are merely venting feelings. The following is a beautiful poem I found that will be profoundly supportive and effectual in connecting with people:

A Poem About Listening

Please, just listen. When I ask you to listen to me, and you start giving advice, you have not done what I asked.

When I ask you to listen to me and you begin to tell me why I shouldn't feel that way, you are trampling on my feelings.

When I ask you to listen to me, and you feel you have to do something to solve my problem, you have failed me, strange as that may seem.

Listen! All I asked was that you listen, not talk, or do...just hear.

Advice is cheap: twenty-five cents will get both Dear Abby and Billy Graham in the same newspaper, and I can do that myself. I'm not helpless.

Maybe discouraged and faltering, but not helpless.

When you do something for me that I can, and need to do for myself, you contribute to my fear and inadequacy.

But when you accept, as a simple fact, that I do feel no matter how irrational, then I can quit trying to convince you and get about the business of understanding what's behind this irrational feeling.

And, when that's clear, the answers are obvious and I don't need advice.

Irrational feelings make sense when we understand what's behind them.

Please listen and just hear me, and if you want to talk wait a minute for your turn, and I'll listen to you.[3]

—Ray Houghton

Listening to people vent their feelings can be especially uncomfortable for many people, and the first inclination is to intervene with their own words to stop the process. The intensity of the other person's outward expression produces anxiety in the listener, and they feel the need to intercept the expression in order to relieve their discomfort. If you feel that temptation, resist it, allow the other person to release his or her feelings; you will be of enormous help to him or her, and your connectedness to that person will be significantly strengthened. It's a small investment—just be there, look that person in the eyes, no effort—it will pay handsome dividends of elevating your influence.

## Rephrase the Content and Reflect the Feeling

The best dialogue I've ever read regarding feelings and giving logical advice comes from Dr. Stephen Covey's book, *The 7 Habits of Highly Effective People*. He describes a conversation between a father and his son who is laboring under some strong anxiety about school. Dr. Covey prefaces the dialogue with the following:

> You can't get him off the phone talking with his friends, but all he gives you is one and two word answers. Your house is a motel where he eats and sleeps, but he never shares, never opens up. And when you think about it, honestly, why should he, if every time he does open up his soft underbelly, you elephant stomp it with autobiographical advice and "I told you so's.

This excellent enlightening dialogue is as follows,

"Boy, Dad, I've really had it! School is for the birds!" *(I want to talk with you, to get your attention)*
"You're feeling frustrated about school" *(That's right! That's how I feel.)*
"I sure am. It's totally impractical. I'm not getting a thing out of it."
"You feel like school's not doing any good." *(Let me think—is that what I mean?)*
"Well, yeah. I'm just not learning anything that's going to help me. I mean, look at Joe. He's dropped out

of school and he's working on cars. He's making money. Now that's practical."

"You feel Joe's really got the right idea." *(Well...)*

"Well, I guess he does in a way. He's really making money now. But in a few years, I bet he'll probably be ticked off at himself"

"You think Joe's going to feel he made the wrong decision."

"He's got to. Just look at what he's giving up. I mean, if you don't have an education, you just can't make it in this world."

"Education is really important."

"Oh, yeah! I mean, if you don't have a diploma, if you can't get jobs or go to college, what are you going to do? You've just got to get an education."

"It's important to your future."

"It is. And...you know what? I'm really worried. Listen, you won't tell Mom, will you?"

"You don't want your mother to find out."

"Well, not really. Oh, I guess you can tell her. She'll probably find out anyway. Look, I took this test today, this reading test. And, dad, they said I'm reading on a fourth grade level. Fourth grade! And I'm a junior in high school!"

What a difference real understanding can make! All the well-meaning advice in the world won't amount to a hill of beans if we're not even addressing the real problem. And we'll never get to the problem if we're so caught up in our own autobiography, our own paradigms, that we don't take off our glasses long enough to see the world from another point of view.

"I'm going to flunk, Dad. I guess I figure if I'm going to flunk, I might as well quit. But I don't want to quit."

"You feel torn. You're in the middle of a dilemma."

"What do you think I should do Dad?"

"Well, I can see some things you might want to consider."

"Like what, Dad?"

"Like getting some special help with your reading. Maybe they have some kind of tutoring program over at the tech school."

"I've already checked into that. It takes two nights and all day Saturday. That would take so much time."

Sensing *emotion* in that reply, the father moves back to *empathy*.

"That's too much of a price to pay."

"Besides, Dad, I told the sixth graders I'd be their coach."

"You don't want to let them down."

"But I'll tell you this, Dad. If I really thought that a tutoring course would help, I'd be down there every night. I'd get someone else to coach those kids"

"You really want the help, but you doubt if the course will make a difference."

"Do you think it would, Dad?"

This father's beautifully skilled responses *rephrased content and reflected feelings,* and as his son grew in confidence of his father's sincere desire to really listen and understand; the barrier between the son's internal turmoil and what's being communicated between the two of them dissipated. This father's communication was accommodated by the elegant use of two tools, *compassion and reason.* When his son was expressing emotion, he used empathy, then, when his son transitioned into logic, he used reason, then, empathy again when the son became emotional. Trust developed, and the son communicates exactly what he's feeling.

This beautiful dialogue Dr. Covey uses, of having the father use empathy and respect for the son's feelings, guided his son's thinking process and resulted in his words reflecting his feelings. The father gave his son the emotional room he needed instead of immediately shooting down his feelings with narrow views of "good sense," allowing his son to use him as a sounding board so as to sort out his emotionalism from his intellect. The father didn't give in to the temptation of immediately giving advise by way of "logic." He used patience and feedback to allow emotional expression, resulting in emotional gratification, helping his son to arrive closer to his own logical conclusion, and, *ask* for his father's opinion. Imagine that, a teenager asking a parent for advice! The miraculous effect of listening.

**Skilled Listening**

Generally, when we think of a good communicator, we think of speaking ability; understandable because we view speaking as active and dynamic, while we may perceive listening as passive and idle. In actuality, listening is quite active and dynamic. When you train yourself to listen with skill, you literally infuse yourself with power that extends into every level of your life. Being tone deaf to what others are trying to communicate becomes detrimental, where relationships falter, families become dysfunctional, millions of dollars in sales are lost, nations enter into war, businesses waver and romance becomes painful.

Of the two-way path by which we communicate, speaking and listening; listening is by far the most underdeveloped; a skill that isn't taught throughout all our school years. In short, when we treat listening as an afterthought, the quality of our lives is diminished. Listening well is work, and well worth the effort because an ability to listen is an ability to be trusted; an ability to listen is an ability to discover; an ability to listen is an ability to control outcomes. Skilled listening enhances your empathy where you become more perceptive in distinguishing peoples' true motives and desires despite what they're saying on the surface.

It's something that has to be practiced, because we think about four times faster than a person can speak, leaving the potential danger for our minds to wander. By far, the greatest enemy in developing this skill of listening is thinking of what you're going to say next while the other person is speaking, and in doing that, you're thinking about the future, you're not in the moment. Living in the moment is where life is. I'm sure you've heard the phrase, the past is dead and the future is an illusion. It's true.

Keeping yourself in the moment while listening provides real opportunity where you can more readily perceive a fleeting opening you would have otherwise missed, along with its potential, which ironically, affects your future. You can be uniquely special if you listen correctly, because most people listen without any intent of understanding; *only with the intent to respond.* Trying to understand someone without listening is like trying to get to the flesh of an apple without cutting its skin. When you're a skilled listener, you suspend your own thoughts, you tune out of your internal dialogue and tune into the person in front of you as he or she speaks. By default, in developing a listening skill, you become less self-centered and more enlightened through other people.

Rather than usually thinking of what to say next, the person you're listening to becomes your guide, directing your response, especially if you're inquisitive.

Another enemy of skilled listening is dismissing a person's intellect as too inferior to utter anything of value, and immediately and silently judging every comment he or she makes without any consideration or curiosity on the merit of its content. Do not allow your first impression of a person to color your judgment of them. Once you let that happen, you will become afflicted with *biased listening,* whereby we "hear" *only what reinforces our first impression.* That's far from skilled listening, that's selective listening. Dale Carnegie, the author of *How to Win friends and Influence People,* offers us this,

> A manager may expect a factory worker to be uneducated and not too bright, so when the worker makes an intelligent and creative suggestion, he does not "hear" it because he cannot believe a good idea can come from that source. Many people, instead of actually hearing what others tell them, hear what their own minds tell them has been said. This is often seen when one has preconceived notions about a person or situation.

Ralph Waldo Emerson said, "Our best thoughts come from others." People drop hints when something is on their minds and they may desire someone to coax it out of them rather than blurt it out. When you're listening well, you will pick up on these subtleties, and exploring them could be extremely beneficial to you in many ways. Not only can it be their personal feelings they might drop hints about, but it could be some news they've had privy to and are reluctant to simply lay on you, so they feel you out with a teaser. I myself have done this several times, and rarely was the other person's listening skills at the level where they picked up on it and drew me out; being too busy with their constant internal dialogue, distracting them from new information. I must say; it's disappointing.

Consequently, if you're off in your own world, you will perhaps miss an outstanding opportunity. Listening pays big. It is a tribute to a person; it is alluring and appreciated. Once you experience its value, that is all the motivation you'll need to fully embrace it, keeping in mind that when you truly listen to a person, it's possible you are the only one who's done so in a long time. That makes you unique, valuable, and special to that individual.

I have had people tell me, "I've never told this to anyone", or, "I don't know why I'm telling you this." Some of these people I hadn't even known very long, as one woman told me this on our first date. Once you open a person up, an avalanche of information could flow from that person, similar to putting a small crack in a dam, and the force of long held pressure precipitates the crack into half the dam falling, surrendering most of its water; you becoming his or her center of attention, his or her focus, and the instrument by which he or she releases expression. In that moment, you become extremely important to that person.

After people express themselves, they are much more receptive to what *you* have to say; their internal dialogue has been quieted, their emotional self has been gratified and they now emotionally allow themselves to concentrate more on *your* thoughts, reciprocating in kind because you have honored their views, sentiments, and feelings. *A good listener is a silent flatterer.*

Skilled listening is like canoeing down a stream, taking in the beautiful scenery as you glide smoothly across its surface watching keenly for side tributaries partly obscured by foliage that will lead you to undiscovered treasure coves—somewhere no one has been before. You will discover the person, and they you. It's an adventure. You're going to enjoy the trip.

## Emotion as Decider

As you can determine by what we've covered so far, the most efficacious path to influencing a person is through his or her feelings. Logic *is* part of the equation, of course, and, the logic you put forth will be far more receptive by the other person when his or her feelings are recognized, acknowledged, and respected. Closeness happens at the level of feeling. Closeness happens when there is discourse of mutual gain, being vigilant to circumvent egos from slipping into the discussion and having it decay into a contest of seemingly logical points, where your listening and questions are executed with caring, curiosity and genuine interest.

The latest research in brain architecture and function has given scientists a more than surprising glimpse of how we all make decisions. They've found that the process of arriving at a decision necessarily utilizes both the rational *and* the emotional parts of the brain. More specifically and significantly, *we cannot make any decisions without the emotional part of the brain.*[4] To me, that is a profound breakthrough in how we interrelate to people. There are scientists who study people with brain injuries, especially in the frontal lobe area, an area that connects with the limbic system (emotional center), and when it's injured, these patients are no longer capable of feeling emotion.

Logic would perhaps tell us that this might enhance their decision-making abilities because the emotional factor is no longer there to "interfere" with the logical process, thereby bringing them to much wiser decisions. We would normally associate emotions with irrational thinking that obscure judgment and distort reasoning, yet paradoxically, the patients' ability to make decisions was severely compromised, and it became problematic to deal with all the pros and cons of everyday issues like what to eat, where to live, etc. These people couldn't bring themselves beyond splitting hairs, obsessing over every bit of minutia and every pro and con—unable to arrive at a decision.

The neurological studies revealed that these patients had both intelligence and memory, but the neural connections that connect the cognitive and emotional centers of the brain were damaged. *With the absence of emotional input, these patients were so overwhelmed by trivial information, that their decision-making processes collapsed, trapped in a perpetual conflict of infinite options.* The emotions operate more in the real world of practicality; they are sensitive to the nuances of life, and it is the *biasing mechanism* we use to *conclude*. Emotions are the management of, and the catalyst to action.

Emotions and logic working together provide us with the ability to choose, rendering us functional for living life in the real world. Our minds are then, efficient mechanisms that necessarily incorporate a blend of both the emotional and rational in order to function successfully in a world of unlimited choices. Without emotions to nudge us off the fence, to be the deciding factor after considering all logical avenues; this new research reveals that we would be caught in a perpetual loop of considering every iota of contrasting data—paralysis by analysis—incompetent to make practical decisions.

As an example, one such patient with frontal lobe damage would take hours to choose a restaurant, fretting over the seating plan, the atmosphere, the menu, and in the end, could not come to a decision. Logic evaluates the hard black-and-white information and all possibilities, it does not, as the frontal lobe patients have experienced and exhibited, have the ability to draw conclusions. It simply provides analysis, and then the emotional aspect of ourselves provides a bias, completing the circuit of arriving at a decision. The rational brain will keep analyzing to the point of paralysis by analysis; the emotional part of ourselves, the limbic system, says, "Hey, hey, c'mon, get with it, let's decide and get on with our lives now;" providing us with a *biasing function*, tipping us off the fence, allowing us to make practical decisions for successful living in the real world. As one neuroscientist expressed it, "Emotion forms the basis for all rational computation—without emotion there is no goal."

This information about human behavior should be recognized as profound and exceedingly valuable. It should excite our sense of the potential for any techniques that take full advantage of how we as human beings work and decide, and greatly help to influence people our way by appealing to the critical emotional factor present in all decision making when seeking cooperation. Recognizing that emotion is the catalyst that makes decisions possible and bringing us to action, we can now approach people with a skill and respect for their humanness that we hitherto lacked. There is an anonymous proverb that says, "Make me feel good and I will produce."

## The Need to Feel Important

Other than survival and the sex drive, psychologists tell us the greatest motivating force in us all is the need to be and feel important. Freud said that everything a person does springs from one of two motives—the sex drive and the desire to be great, and Dr. Alfred Adler says that man wants most of all to be significant. The father of psychology, William James states, "The deepest principle in human nature is the craving to be appreciated." Dr. John Dewey said, "The deepest urge of all in human nature is the desire to be important."

Therefore, anything we can do to help people gain a feeling of more significance and importance, will aid us in our quest for their heartfelt cooperation, and why most of the techniques we'll cover speak to this need. In business for example, it could be as simple as recognition. It doesn't have to be a parade and a five-foot trophy; it could be praise during a meeting, a plaque, an e-mail, a call, a lunch, or a note. Some may fear giving recognition will give workers license to become prima-donnish, sit back... relax; but then, it's hard to sit back when you've been infused with energy induced by a heightened feeling of self-worth.

Consider the possibility that your work environment may be the only place where some or many of your workers receive any kind of recognition and appreciation, and socially, or in family life, making a person feel important can be as simple as greeting them with enthusiasm. Doing this to children can be life-altering. It can infuse wonderful healing feelings into anyone when they feel genuinely valued, Stephen Covey calls it psychic compensation, many times, more valued and motivational than financial compensation.

Visualize it, what would you feel in response to a caring enthusiastic greeting accompanied with a wide smile when you walked into a room, solely on the strength of your presence? You have the power to bestow that on people. In his book, *Van Fleet's Master Guide for Managers,* Jim Van Fleet reports on a study conducted by a team of psychologists from the University of Missouri. Conducting two tests, they determined the relative merits of praise versus criticism with army recruits given difficult tasks, and divided into six squads of ten men each. They tested three thousand men. The results were as follows:

| Squad# | Critique Method | Percent Showing Improvement on Second Test |
|---|---|---|
| 1 | Public Praise | 90% |
| 2 | Private Praise | 75% |
| 3 | Private Criticism | 49% |
| 4 | Public Criticism | 31% |
| 5 | Private Ridicule | 19% |
| 6 | Public Ridicule | 10% |

Energy. The leader giveth or taketh. Energizing the workforce would be *the* thing...the first thing any leader would want to do. *Recognition* then, is hands down the most powerful tool a manger has to energize his or her workforce, therefore, promoting cooperation. Much too often though, it's treated as an afterthought or not at all. In our social relationships, that energy will forge closeness, directing the relationship where we want it to go. Recognition then, is simply a feeling we can implant into whomever we wish, the feeling of importance. As Dr. Wayne Dyer encourages, "Catch someone doing something right."

As a person who reveres logic, truth, and common sense, I am still cognizant of the intellect that feelings have to offer. Both logic and feelings are to be equally valued in navigating more successfully through life. In his book, *The Art of Thinking,* Thomas Sharper Knowlson enlightens us with these eloquent words,

> Those who boast that they are the disciples of pure reason, and sneer at the poor 'emotionalist,' are debtors to emotion far beyond their knowledge.

## The Feeling that Saved the World

It was September 26, 1983, about half passed midnight in Russia; it was September 25, 1983 in the United States, on a Sunday afternoon. Deep inside Serpukhov-15, a secret bunker of Russia's Ballistic Missile Early Warning System command and control post deep in a forest thirty-miles northeast of Moscow, deafening alarms were suddenly tripped via their satellite warning system, picking up a flash in Montana near a Minuteman II silo. Sirens were blaring, warning lights were flashing and screens showing an unbelievably nightmarish horror show of one, then two, then three and finally five nuclear missiles speeding toward Russia at about 15,000 miles an hour.

Amid this were 120 panicked military officers and engineers sitting behind their terminals, then jumping from their seats to focus on one man whose role it was to evaluate incoming data, having less than fifteen minutes to decide whether or not to press the red button flashing the word "START" in bright lettering; initiating a retaliation against America, which would without doubt, literally transform the face of the planet. Two countries would incinerate each other in one hour and radioactive fallout and a nuclear winter would bring to an end the world, as we know it. The man is 44 year-old Lieutenant Colonel Stanislav Petrov. Unbelievably, most of the world has never heard of him.

Just three weeks before, the Soviet military accidentally shot down a Korean Airline Flight 007 killing 269 people including many Americans, and President Reagan denounced the Soviet Union as an "evil empire." In the same year President Reagan made his Star Wars speech stoking fear in the Soviets that such new technology would increase the chance of America launching a first strike, along with the ability to intercept a Soviet retaliation.

Also, the United States was about to deploy the Pershing II missile that could hit Moscow from West Germany in twelve minutes; there was a series of psychological naval maneuvers by the West into Soviet strategic areas like the submarine bases in the Barents Sea, and the United States and NATO were involved in exercises known as Able Archer, using tactical nuclear weapons in Europe that put Soviet leaders on edge, fearing it was a cover for an invasion.[5]

With all this history, the Soviets were on hair trigger alert. Both sides comprising a grotesque gigantic war machine poised to blow-up the planet on a moments notice, setting the stage for a perceived first strike, and setting off cascading events that would end in Armageddon.

Petrov, trained as a scientist, was under enormous stress beyond all imagination. He recalls, his legs were "like cotton." With a phone in one hand and an intercom in the other, while electronic maps and consoles were flashing, he was trying to digest all the information at once, "Everyone jumped from their seats looking at me. What could I do? There was a procedure that I had written myself." Although he had a gnawing feeling the computer system was wrong, he had no way of knowing for sure.

The ground radar units that were controlled from a different command center could not verify the attack because they were incapable of seeing beyond the horizon. He knew the system had flaws, "I just couldn't believe that just like that, all of a sudden, someone would hurl five missiles at us. The U.S. had not five, but a thousand missiles in battle readiness." But the protocol dictated, as did his orders, that he press the red button, automatically engaging an irretrievable launching sequence of a full-scale nuclear war, all 5,000 of their missiles against the United States.

Petrov says, "The main computer wouldn't ask me, it was made so that it wouldn't even ask. It was specially constructed in such a way that no one could affect the system's operations." His paranoid superiors

repeatedly told him that the United States would launch a massive attack against them. Despite all these factors racing through his mind, Petrov relates,
   "I had a funny feeling in my gut."

He agonizingly decides it's a false alarm. So he and the crew waited. Seconds passed. Then minutes...twenty agonizing minutes passed. All was quiet. He was right. He averted an all-out nuclear war and everyone around him congratulated him for his superb judgment; there he stood; a hero of unprecedented proportions.

   What had happened was the false alarm came from a satellite. Shortly after midnight, the sun, the satellite system and the United States missile fields all lined up in such a way as to maximize the sunlight reflected from high-altitude clouds in Montana, giving an appearance of several missiles in flight. The most disquieting and chilling thing about this entire story is that Stanislav Petrov was not originally scheduled to be on duty that evening; the person originally scheduled called in ill and Petrov had to work a double shift.

   There is little doubt that another commanding officer, given the high-alert itchy-trigger paranoia of the higher echelon, would have followed protocol. The normal officer in a command post is not a scientist, and he follows check lists scrupulously, and does not deviate. They trust their equipment and do not want to make any decisions, especially one of that magnitude, and the results would have been monumentally and horrifically different.

   Stanislav Petrov retired in 1993 to care for his wife suffering from a brain tumor. He now lives in a small village near Moscow, living on $200 a month pension. He was neither rewarded nor honored for his actions, rather, he was inflicted with intense questioning by his superiors because he disobeyed military procedure. They didn't punish him, but his promising military career ended.

We almost died in 1983. The world owes him big. In 2006, this forgotten hero was honored at a special ceremony in the Dag Hammarskjold auditorium at the United Nations in New York City. Stanislav Petrov spoke there and was presented with a World Citizen Trophy by the Association of World Citizens. His heroism has earned him the title of *The Man Who Averted Nuclear War*. In his small apartment while making tea during an interview, he said, "I was simply a person doing my job." His inner intelligence, *a feeling*, was one of greatest gifts ever bestowed upon humanity. We thank you Stanislav, from the bottom of our hearts for listening to your inner voice.


Respecting peoples' feelings will be of immense value in our cooperative effort, and valuing the intelligence of our inner voice and that of others heightens our competency. When used in concert with recognizing and analyzing the facts, it can aid us enormously when confronted with difficult decisions.

# Strategies of Influence
# Though Emotional Connection

*People want to be appreciated not impressed.*
*They want to be regarded as human beings,*
*not as mere sounding boards for other*
*peoples' egos. They want to be treated as*
*ends in themselves, not as a means toward*
*the gratification of another's vanity.*
—Sydney J. Harris

*Life does not happen to us, it happens from us.*
—Michael Wickett


## Setting the Stage

All the techniques and concepts presented in this book are reliant and built upon a foundation of courtesy and respect toward the people whose cooperation you're attempting to enlist, without which, renders them all much less effective. Voluntary cooperation can only be achieved if these two elements are created, honored, and most importantly, perceived. As obvious as this premise may seem, it is so vitally important, it's worth establishing from the start. From this vital connection we can then develop the powerful springboard—trust.

Cooperation *is* possible without trust as long as there isn't mistrust, however, if you set up trust as a condition beforehand, you're in a far more powerful position to attain compliance. There is probably no substitute for developing a sincere concern for other people when you are speaking with them, so to the extent that you can cultivate this within yourself will be directly proportional to your success with people and relationships. This is definitely a win/win proposition.

All the techniques we discuss will be far easier to execute if you own this sincerity. You will be more relaxed when you're conversing and you will see greater success, therefore motivating you forward to continue developing empathy. As a result of coming from a place of sincerity and concern, your small physical movements called "tells," a term used in playing poker, will change. These "tells" can signal to the other person if you're sincere or indifferent, whether or not you have another agenda going on in your mind—an ulterior motive. These "tells" are powerful, caused by neural activities of which you are utterly unaware. In fact, as neuroscience tells us, a person looking at your face and listening to the tone of your voice is many times more aware of your internal motivations than you are.

Ninety-three percent of communications is nonverbal, and much of that amount is through body language. Our emotions are mirrored through our facial expressions, which has now become an actual science pioneered by psychologist Paul Eckman. He has studied emotions for more than forty years, focusing mainly on how facial expressions reveal them. He's filmed a multitude of peoples' faces across the world and has mapped the muscular structure of the face in how they form expressions—the seven main ones are; happiness, sadness, agony, fear, surprise, contempt and disgust.

These movements and expressions have been computerized and represented in complex graphs where scientists can determine the emotions they represent. Facial expression and body language are excellent representations of the proverbial mind-body connection at work, and we are all pretty good at reading them both on a conscious and unconscious level. The emotions control all these movements and unless you are very practiced, where you are consciously and consistently monitoring your every movement and expression, they most likely will belie your words if you're insincere.

If there is a disconnect between what you're saying and your feelings, there's a good chance it will be reflected outwardly and perceived by the person or persons you're speaking to. They may not be able to put their finger on it, yet they will be nudged by the intellect of their feelings, and the force of what you're attempting to communicate to them will be diluted, along with your ability to influence them..

Signaling impatience and boredom is another deal-spoiler. When you're impatient, you give off those little "tells". It could be body language, darting your eyes back and forth to something else in the room and back to the person, or fiddling with something, etc.

This signal will undermine the other person's sense of your sincerity, the message being, I don't want to be here with you and I can't wait for this conversation to be over so I can get you out of my hair. Bad start. I had a sales manager who I liked, but many times he would execute an impatient "tell" and I picked it up every time loud and clear. In the course of conversation, he would take a deep breath where I could see his chest rise and fall, coupled with the laborious look in his eyes giving me a sense of his being concerned only for himself and of being used. Doesn't feel good.

Cooperation is an automatic byproduct of trust, and the shortest, quickest and easiest path to the true spirit of cooperation. We align our thinking with anyone in whom we trust because we feel they are in alliance with what's in our own best interest. It's important to realize that exhibiting trust *in* another is an excellent way to *be* trusted. For example, a manager who delegates important tasks to his most able people will be trusted more than a manager who consistently has his hands in the details. The latter manager's staff will feel he's competing with them and he'll probably lose his most competent employees, retaining the people who don't mind relaxing while he does the work.

Your integrity, or at least the perception of your integrity, is the key to establishing trust with others. The word integrity is often used loosely. It *does* mean something, especially today in our steroid-paced society, where people hunger for this trait and are impressed when they find it, because of its rarity. Practicing it then will no doubt bring people to place their trust in us and bring their cooperation with it as well. It's an excellent foundation. Practicing it is somewhat simple; a small investment with high dividends.

First, be a person *Of Your Word*. You want the people around you to know and feel that when you say something, they can take it to the bank. If you say you're going to do something, *do it*. If you're not going to do it, *don't say it*. If you say you're going to be somewhere, *be there*. If you say you'll have something done by a certain time, *have it at that time or before*. If you can't deliver, *say you can't*. When you or your company performs the inevitable screw-up, and that injured irate client, or irate social acquaintance is trying to reach you, *face up to it immediately*.

If it turns out that you're wrong about something, command respect by having the strength of character and emotional security to say straight up, *"I was wrong,"* instead of delivering a verbal tap dance in a pathetic attempt to squirm out of it. This type of behavior is a rare commodity in our modern fast-paced world, and since it's in short supply, it creates a high demand. *You* can be that rarity, and *choose* to possess it. People say a lot of things...they talk-the-talk but rarely walk-the-walk.

Who among us doesn't despise the businessperson or politician who will say anything to get you to act in his or her favor, or the "friend", beside you only when you're riding high, or the romantic other who espouses words of love and behaves with the opposite actions. A person whose word is golden is something we all value, and we can be exactly *that* to other people.

In the previous chapter we discussed how we all, as human beings, have a need to feel important, and a simple strategy to induce this feeling into others is to sincerely ask for their input and their advice. In my days of sales management it would be common for me to ask my staff either individually or as a group when wrestling with a problem, "What do you think?" I could feel the positive impact of how it made them feel about themselves, and in their feeling of a close relationship with me; so, a strategy we could use when seeking the cooperation others, is ask them for their advice on something, say a few days before you attempt to enlist their cooperation. This will go far in priming their minds, and help to weaken any resistance they may have to the idea you want to present to them.

I once heard a story about a manager who used an excellent similar method. He would go to his people for suggestions, let's say, on how to reduce overhead. The great majority of the time they would be creative and offer workable solutions. From there it was on automatic pilot because he then merely asked them to implement their own suggestions. He used this method because *people will always support their own ideas*. It doesn't get more beautiful than that.

Emotionally, it's almost impossible for people to contribute one hundred percent of their effort if they are not allowed to have their ideas considered. The fact is, that employees who are forbidden to express their voices do less work than those whose suggestions are embraced. This concept applies not only to business it applies to all areas of life as a fundamental human response. Getting the family together for a family problem solving conference would be an excellent way to have all members voice their opinion as to how to solve problems and; to make improvements.

This concept is extremely powerful because even when the parents finally make a ruling, it is willingly to accepted because the children had the opportunity to voice their opinions. The psychology of asking people or family members, etc. how they would solve a particular problem, engages a response that seems to *make the problem theirs also*, and, their appropriate response is to try and solve it, many times with pride and gratification. It again must be emphasized, that when applying this technique, or any other for that matter, of asking for advice, sincerity is crucial.

Everybody brings their own brand of life's experiences to the table, and one or two words from their perspective could be the catalyst that opens your eyes to a wonderful solution. If there is even a hint of disingenuousness, of patronizing them, you will shoot yourself in both feet. Respect their intelligence.

Being aware that your ego will affect those around you and will be of enormous value in how they respond to you. The indulged ego can reduce an otherwise highly intelligent person into behaving in ways that are unbelievably counterproductive to their own best interests, whereby it distracts them from what's going on around them, away from reality, and taming it will allow them to function much more effectively for themselves and others. We will delve much deeper into this crucial subject in the next chapter.

**The Pygmalion Effect:** In acquiring cooperation, it is extremely helpful to be aware that the world around us reacts to *us* much more than we realize. We, of course, in the heat of everyday life, feel we are reacting to the world; yet each of us possess a great amount of power in influencing people as to how they respond to us, and, as to how they feel about themselves. In 1968, the psychologist Robert Rosenthal and the principal of an elementary school, Lenore Jacobson conducted a famous study that is known today as the Pygmalion effect,[1] also known as a self-fulfilling prophecy. They were concerned that the teachers' *expectations* of lower-class and minority children were a serious factor in the high failure rates of these children.

The study received its name from a story Ovid told from the tenth book of Metamorphoses about the sculptor Pygmalion, a prince of Cyprus. Pygmalion wanted to create an ivory statue of the ideal, most desirable woman whom he called Galatea. When he finished, the ivory statue was so beautiful Pygmalion fell madly in love with his creation and so desperate was he to have her, prayed to the goddess Aphrodite to breath life into Galatea. Aphrodite granted his wish, and united Pygmalion and Galatea into marriage where they lived happily ever after.

The hypothesis of Rosenthal's study was to test if children would become brighter when *they were expected to*, by their teachers. The study was conducted in eighteen primary school classes in a predominantly lower class but not impoverished community. They informed the teachers that they would test students to determine their intelligence quotients (IQs) and that the test will also will identify those students who would make accelerated and above-average intellectual progress in the coming year, even if they were now less than good students. Then, before the next school year started, teachers received the names of the students who, on the basis of the test, would be expected to perform higher than the others.

Twenty percent of the students were chosen to be the "brighter" children. In actuality, Rosenthal and Jacobson had randomly picked the names from the class list. Any difference between these children and the rest of the class existed only in the minds of the teachers. Then, a real IQ test was administered at the end of the year to determine the effect, if any. The students who had been identified as "academic spurters" showed on average, over a 12 point increase on their IQ scores, compared to an increase of 8 points for the rest of the students. The differences were even larger in the earlier grades, with almost half of the first and second-grade spurters showing an increase of 20 points or more.

The teachers also indicated that these "special" students were more well behaved, more intellectually inquisitive and were friendlier than the other students. Rosenthal and Jacobson concluded that a self-fulfilling prophecy was at work here. The study showed that when teachers' attitudes are influenced, they induce a *strong interpersonal effect* toward the students, thereby creating the Pygmalion effect; subtly, powerfully, and unconsciously producing the performance they expected to see by their changed attitude toward, and expectations of, the children.

Not only did they spend more time with these children, they were also more enthusiastic about teaching them, unintentionally showing and exuding more warmth toward them than the other children. These chosen children *felt* more capable and intelligent and they performed accordingly, just on the weight of the teachers' expectations of them. Rosenthal expands further on the findings of the study stating,

> [W]e gave each of the teachers in the school the names of a handful of children in her classroom that would get smart in the academic year ahead. These kids' names were taken out of a hat. We chose them by means of a table of random numbers. The children themselves did not know in any direct way that teachers were holding certain expectations for them. Teachers were told not to tell the kids and of course we didn't tell the children either. So the children never knew. In effect, a double blind study.
>
> And then when we tested the children a year later, we found that those kids who'd be allegedly to their teachers be showing or going to show intellectual gains, in fact showed greater intellectual gains than did the children of whom we'd said nothing in particular. So the kids actually got smarter

when they were expected to get smarter by their teachers.

We've come to feel that there are really four factors that operate in the mediation or communication of these self-fulfilling prophecies, especially in a classroom *but not only in a classroom.* So what are these four things that teachers tend to do differently to kids for whom they have more favorable expectations?

The first factor is the *climate* factor. Teachers tend to create a warmer climate for those children for whom they have more favorable expectations. They are nicer to them, both in terms of the things they say and also in the non-verbal channels of communication. The other very important factor is the so-called *input* factor. That one probably won't surprise anyone. Teachers teach more material to those kids for whom they [have] more favorable expectations. After all, if you think a kid is dumb and can't learn you are not going to put yourself out to try to teach him very much.

Two other factors though make a difference. One is the *response opportunity* factor, that is kids get more of a chance to respond if the teachers expect more of them. They call on them more often and when they do call on them they let them talk longer and they help and shape with them the answers that the kids speak out—kind of working together to put the response out.

The last is *feedback*. The feedback factor works in this way: As you might expect if more is expected of the kid, the kid is praised more, positively reinforced more for getting a good answer out, but interestingly enough is given more differentiated feedback when they get the wrong answer.

One of the ways in which you can sometimes tell a little bit that the teacher does not have very high expectations for a kid is that the teacher is willing to accept a low quality response or won't really clarify what would have been a good quality response. Maybe because he or she feels, "Well what's the use, the kid is not smart enough to profit from this additional clarification."

So those are the four factors; *climate, input, response opportunity, and feedback.*"

The implications of the Pygmalion effect are profound and more far-reaching than that of teaching children. It also reaches leaders, team members, parents and family members. It means that *the cooperation, performance and attitude of the person and people you interact with depends in large part upon you.* Consciously or unconsciously, we cue people as to what our expectations are. In other words, what we communicate is what we get. We communicate innumerable cues and "tells" that people perceive, whereby they then carry out the self-fulfilling prophecies we have created for them.

Once an expectation is set, even if it's inaccurate, people strongly tend to act in ways that are consistent with that expectation. Examining the four factors of climate, input, response opportunity and feedback, and analyzing how we perform them in our own environments, will most likely make a massive difference in other peoples' behavior, just as it did with the students. As Johann Goethe offered,

> If we take people as we find them we may make them worse, but if we treat them as though they are what they should be, we help them to become what they are capable of becoming.

**Employee or Member Dossier**: If you are a manager or an owner of a company, a leader in an organization or a member of a team, you may want to consider utilizing an *Employee or Member Dossier*. The illustration on the next page is a guide that you can customize to your preferences. I used this tool in the sales field for clients and prospects in giving me an edge over competition. It is one of the most powerful tools I've ever used in bringing me emotionally closer to people. It works this way: after you have a conversation with your employee or associate and learn a tidbit of information about him or her, enter it later on a pre-made form that you've designed. For example you may have learned that one of your employee's children are named Jerry and Susie. You enter it into your form and refer to it before you speak to that person again and can ask about his children by name.

Another example is, your associate mentioned his wife is about to graduate from Cornel University with a Masters degree in Hotel Administration. You merely enter it in his dossier. When you meet with him again you can ask about her graduation, because the dossier you reviewed beforehand reminded you about it. It's a customized rapport builder. Remember to enter the date each time you enter information; this will tell you when you last entered new information, reminding you to learn more if it's been a long while since you've updated it.

This is a first rate technique, tailored to get next to people emotionally. The small amount of time taken to develop these dossiers is one of the best investments you'll ever make in reaching out and touching your employees or members and will act like WD-40 when gaining their visceral cooperation. With this technique, we also initiate what is known as the *rule of reciprocity*. It states that if I give you something you will feel obligated to give me something back, which is a response we've all been psychologically conditioned to respond to—no one likes deadbeats or people that are selfish.

The dossier is tailor-made to do exactly that. Remembering their children's names, birthdays or their anniversaries with a card or just by mentioning it, as an example, triggers the reciprocity response, and will be instrumental toward compliance when you request their cooperation. The rule of reciprocity is a powerful tool because it is emotionally ingrained into most, if not all cultures. People are inclined to repay in kind.

# Johnny Smith

Update Date: August, 18, 2011

Home address:  Jamestown

Company:  Barnes & Barnes

Previous company:  Bantam Publishing

Degree:  English

School:  University of Illinois

Activities:  Racquetball

Interests:  Cooking

Years married:

Religion:

Political orientation:

Birthday:  September, 5

Anniversary:

Previous marriage:

Children's names::  Jerry, Susie

Birth dates:

Activities:  Jerry, soccer

Spouse's name:  Gloria

Company:

Degree:  MA Hotel Administration

School:  Cornel University

Activities:  Tennis

Interests:

Notes:

## Techniques

**Assign a virtue:** There is an inordinately powerful mechanism that is rarely used to engender true communication in the quest for compliance. Like many potent techniques, it's quite simple—tell the person how to respond. This may sound strange, so let's look at the way Winston Churchill expressed it,

> I have found that the best way to get another to acquire a virtue, is to impute it to him.

As an example, if you want to increase the odds of getting the truth from someone, you will assign the virtue of truth to that individual before you ask your question, "John, I need to ask you something. I'm asking *you* because I feel you are a truthful person and someone who has the courage to look me in the eye and say it like it is; someone who doesn't spread a falsehood." Then ask your question.

How could that person not live up to the standard you just set for him? You can supplant any virtue you're after into the other person. If you're working toward a cooperative union, the virtue would be, "You're someone who looks objectively at a situation, assesses it and is instrumental in arriving at a positive solution." Then state your case and request his cooperation. Any one of us would be hard pressed not to live up to being that person. We all want to be better people and to be recognized as such.

This approach offers a person the opportunity to *be* a better person, and most of us will gladly seize that opportunity. It is wonderfully effective, just as long as you don't convey a sense of manipulation.

**Explain why:** In approaching and enlisting a person's help and cooperation, another potently effective technique is to take the time to explain *why*. It has many excellent benefits. Explaining why you want something done, especially if it's in the business environment, automatically removes the curse of bossiness. When there's a good reason why something ought to be done, it puts you in the position of simply making a logical request, completely removing the bad taste that comes from being ordered around.

If it's in a social setting, explaining why carries with it a message of respect. Professor of psychology at *Harvard*, Ellen Langer, performed a famous study called, *The Copy Machine*.[2] Professor Langer and her researchers conducted this study in the Graduate Center at the City University of New York, where they asked people waiting in line at a copy machine if they could use the machine first. Each time, they asked one of three questions. One asked, "Excuse me, may I use the Xerox machine?" Sixty percent allowed them to go ahead.

When they were asked, "Excuse me, may I use the Xerox machine because I'm in a rush," ninety-five per cent allowed them to use the copy machine, and surprisingly when they were asked, "May I use the copy machine because I have to make some copies," the result still remained at almost 95 per cent. Interestingly, whether the reason given was sensible or nonsensical, there was substantially more cooperation than when a reason was not offered, indicating that merely the structure of giving a reason is why the people were much more compliant to the requests.[7]

It seems that since the word "because" is usually followed by information, it has become a programmed response—a trigger— that incites a "yes" response despite offering a flimsy reason. Of course there's a limit to the silliness one offers, yet the fact remains that making an effort to explain why using the word "because" is extremely effective.

When you explain why, you also lessen the chances of error. People who understand why they're doing something are less apt to foul it up, and if the situation changes so that the action is no longer required, they'll have sense enough to stop. If they don't understand the purpose of the request, they'll have no choice but to blindly go ahead doing what you asked them to do. Also, explaining the reason for your request is a compliment to the people you've asked to carry it out, showing that you think it's important that they should understand what they're doing and be able to use their heads. You also put them in a gratifying position to make suggestions, which obviously would be helpful to your cause. Moreover, to top it all off, this technique will engender and cultivate trust.

**Excellent communication:** Communication enhances cooperation. In the course of conversation if a person blurts something out that seems irrelevant to the discussion at hand, it doesn't necessarily mean his thought processes are breaking down. It means that there's a deeper undercurrent of feelings and ideas that are simultaneous at play within him. As mentioned in chapter one, there are two elements of excellent communication—*sequence of logic based on the facts and to satisfy emotional needs*, therefore a good communicator will allow for this by encouraging the person to vent his or her feelings, or expand upon his or her path of thought.

As we covered earlier, this gives people an opportunity to gain something from the dialogue, and of course, moves them forward toward a cooperative state of mind. Resistance has both rational and irrational elements. When resistance is brought up into conversation, the rational will usually maintain its integrity and, over time, the irrational element at the conversational level will have a tendency to dissolve, indicating that irrational resistance has much more power in the recesses of a person's mind than it does at the surface and expression of dialogue.

This is probably one of the most difficult aspects to keep in mind when dealing with irrationality and to exercise patience. We all tend to become annoyed and exasperated when irrational views are thrown at what we feel are our logical and well thought out ideas and where we must then enter battle and thwart that ghoul with force and expediency. Admittedly, I have been guilty of this more times than I can count. It's something we must continually work on. The technique previously discussed of *rephrasing the content and reflecting the feeling* is especially effective in mitigating irrationality because when you function as a sounding board for this person by reflecting his or her thoughts back to this person, it provides the opportunity for him or her to assess more objectively what he or she just said—and now heard—and likely to sound just as irrational to that person as it did to you; especially if there's a hesitation after you reflect the feeling back. Even if it's prolonged; *do not interrupt*—listen, they are reprocessing their position.

Encouraging people to vent their feelings is easily accomplished by drawing them out through questions, and, armed with skillful listening, questions become a natural byproduct, helping enormously toward harmonious communication. It may be appropriate to begin with simple, easy questions that could be answered with "yes" or "no." Then once the person is more at ease and comfortable, move on to questions that are known as open-ended questions, that is, questions that start with *how, what*, and *why*.

These questions direct the person to talk *about* a particular subject, rather than merely provide certain facts, where his or her answers will then guide and navigate you through the dialogue to get where you want to go, again, provided you are listening skillfully. You are definitely on the right track if the person is spending more time talking than you are. That's a barometer you want to be aware of always. *If you're working harder than the other person is, you're going in the wrong direction when drawing someone out*. Excellent communication occurs when you fall out of love with your own voice. If an individual is somewhat reluctant to talk, be patient, it's conversational inertia. Once a person starts speaking, he or she probably will be just as reluctant to stop.

Another invaluable technique in communication is to summarize back your understanding of the essence of her words and concept utilizing the technique we covered earlier of *rephrasing the content and reflect the feeling*. If she agrees, the answer will be yes, if she disagrees, she now is faced with something of an open-ended question where she's compelled to explain and clarify her position and you will receive new information. Further, have your radar up for any extraneous comments that seem to be off the logical train of thought or if an unrelated subject is introduced into the dialogue.

*A pause in the conversation allows for the to think about the reply*

Explore this line of thought and determine why this individual introduced the topic. This will go a long way in connecting both your thinking and bringing you closer together. Be aware *that irrelevancy is an appeal for expressing emotional needs*...if your rational mind becomes exasperated and immediately challenges and halts that line of thought and expression, you will lose important emotional leverage with that person. I have also been guilty of *this* many times; something I struggle with and need to constantly work on. Recognize this as an opportunity to give this person a *gain* from the conversation, and you will also gain in winning her cooperation.

Viewing irrelevancy as an opportunity rather than an irritant will give you another powerful tool to win cooperation. People want to be reminded that others care about them, and approve of them so they don't feel isolated, therefore, taking a little detour during the conversation is to pick up big dividends. Perhaps a few exploratory detours are in order, but the odds of you getting to your objective are much greater than insisting on a straight-line, impatient, no-nonsense path. A no-nonsense path may give *you* emotional gratification, but you may well trade in your major objective for *it*. Don't trade the war for the battle.

In your dialogue, one excellent technique during your conversation that will pay off handsomely is to pause briefly before replying to something they've said or to a question they've asked. This pause strongly communicates to the person to whom you're speaking that you are absorbing her thoughts and formulating an appropriate reply. To answer instantly sends a strong message that you have a pre-formulated knee-jerk response, and, were probably not even listening. The

*+ also to take the to digest their ~~feelings~~ thoughts*

pause extends courtesy and respect—the foundation of communication and cooperation—by implying her idea has merit and worthy of consideration, thereby cultivating and nurturing her receptivity to your idea. Listening is an art, it is a giving, and a much greater power than most realize—far greater than words.

**Assurance phrases:** In the field of sales there is a potent tool used in the process of persuasion known as assurance phrases. Assurance phrases are those phrases that are used immediately after you encounter a verbal response of resistance. The assurance phrase buffers your response to the other person, avoiding the discussion from precipitating into a mild debate where you will end up DOA. It also validates the feelings of the person's view, helping to give you an opportunity to skillfully neutralize it. Here are some assurance phrases:

      *a.* That's a good point
      *b.* I never considered that before
      *c.* That's true
      *d.* I can understand that
      *e.* That's a perfectly natural reaction
      *f.* You're right
      *g.* You have a right to feel that way
      *h.* That's the best way I've ever heard that point stated

For example, you want to go and see a movie about World War II with your girlfriend and she objects with, "There are so many war movies, I'm tired of them...besides they make me uncomfortable." Your response with an assurance phrase might be,

> Yes, *I can understand you feeling that way* Valerie. I wouldn't want you be uncomfortable. There *are* a lot of war movies...I just thought this particular movie would give me a lot of insight into why it happened. It's an important part of our history...and I wanted to share it with you.

As you can see, her feelings are validated and respected, harmonizing with her energy, and then expressed how you feel. Chances are much greater she will agree to go with you. There are many more assurance phrases, and you can create your own. Through practice, these have to be second nature to you so you're able to use them automatically.

Another example, Susan works for the Big Brothers program where men volunteers give about a half-a-day a week for a commitment of one year to spend constructive time with a boy who doesn't have a father; helping nurture that boy through a difficult part of life. Susan has a friend who would be an outstanding match for a certain boy. Approaching her friend, she tells him about the boy and because she knows of his sensitivity to, and compassion for people, asks him for his participation. He balks, and seems reluctant with that much of a commitment saying,

"I don't know, I've never considered myself as a father figure and, well, it seems daunting."

Susan responds, "Michael, *you're absolutely right*. It *is* a great responsibility and I know what I'm asking of you, and it's precisely the reason I thought of you; *because* of your responsible nature. You would be able to relate to this boy so well and be an excellent influence in his life. We really need people who approach this with exactly that attitude."

Here again, we see that she has harmonized with his emotions and then gently moved his attention to her cause, bringing him closer to complying with it.

**Lose the But:** A cardinal rule, is to never ever use the word "but" after an assurance phrase. "But" actually will negate the assurance phrase, being an eraser word, inferring everything you said before "but" was disingenuous, and smacks of a competitive mild debate. We all can sense when someone is about to unload that word on us, waiting with baited breath for the next sentence to drop—I love you too *but*, you're a great guy *but*, it's a good idea *but*, well I would love to go skydiving with you *but,* I want to get married too, *but,* etc. Instead of but, replace it with *and* or *also,* or just go to another sentence.

Instead of, "That's a good idea, but..." you can say,

"That's a good idea Jerry. Another idea I had..."

Or, "That's a good idea, and another one is..."

An excellent phrase that can replace "but," is, *having said that*. For example, "Your idea is a great solution and I can see you've put quite a bit of thought into it, *having said that*, I'd like to point out that..." "But" is a word you should remove from your vocabulary when used in this context. You'll have to concentrate to eliminate the word "but" because it rolls off the tongue so easily. It's used much too often for no good reason.

**Tell a story:** Telling a story about yourself helps you *relate* to the other person. In sales it's known as *the third party story*. Telling a story provides an *open sesame* doorway to the emotional attention of the listener. It has the unique ability to draw someone into your words and thoughts on a visceral level, enhancing greatly the person's interest because it's a story—a story flows, unlike espousing a series of facts; it is like the difference between a slide show and a feature film on the screen of the mind. Delivering the third party story is an art. You can create as much drama and emotion as you wish to engage and capture another's mind.

This means you listen for anything in their conversation that is similar to your experiences, or experiences that people close to you have had. For example, let us say the person inadvertently says that she is caring for an aging parent in her home. You draw her out by asking about it. Then if you've had, or are having the same experience, you relate with her on that subject. You then offer the experience,

> You know, like with your situation, my father lived with us. He was ill with diabetes and a heart condition. He was so weak he couldn't walk up a few stairs to the bedroom, so we had to carry him. Since both my wife and I worked, we had to hire a caregiver during the day to care and cook for him. We even had to get an oxygen machine for him. It's never easy when a parent becomes that dependent on you. And there's no doubt that it's harder on the parent in that they suffer from the feeling of being a burden on their children, on top of losing their independence.

At that moment you become human in his or her eyes. You and this person are alike at some level, and you now carry more influence with this person; so be aware, listen, and *relate* with the person you're interfacing with. Additionally, you can elevate this to an even more powerful level. In the discourse of relating, if you can both *complain* about a common issue supporting each other's feelings, you're now walking with arms around each other's shoulders with a shared gripe, aligned together toward a common enemy. Both of you, now allies, are even closer emotionally. It's powerful. If you cannot think of a story, *relating* itself still remains a potent technique, therefore, keep your antennae up for opportunities in your conversation where you share similarities, and point them out, such as interests, people you both may know, hobbies, same school, children, etc. The list is endless.

**In their best interest:** Another effective way in which to enlist cooperation from a person or group, is demonstrating to them that it's in their best interest to sign for two reasons.

> First, how they would profit from the cooperative effort.
> Second, the loss will they incur if they do not.

I had an interesting experience once when shopping for a painting at an art sale. As my wife and I were browsing the dozens of pictures hanging on the walls, we were passing by a man and a salesman standing in front of a painting.

The salesman was obviously trying to sell it to the man who seemed somewhat interested but was hesitant. As we passed by I happened to glance at the painting, and I liked it a lot and said to my wife, "That's a beautiful picture." The man heard my comment, turned and looked at me with what I would describe as a look of both being threatened and violated...how dare I infringe on his maybe property. Within fifteen seconds he purchased the painting, and if he hadn't, he sensed quite accurately, I would have. I was kicking myself for opening my yap.

At the moment I made that comment, he emotionally experienced a potential loss that immediately moved him into compliance, and I knocked him off the fence for the salesman; I should have asked for part of his commission. Using information to point out a potential loss to someone is not to be confused with crude hysterical scare tactics, such as, "You'll lose everything," "This is the worst thing you can do," or those used in the political arena with accusations of nazism, communism, socialism, terrorism, warnings of mushroom clouds and death panels. Using scare tactics like these are underhanded and painfully obvious unsophisticated ploys, therefore, ineffective when dealing with savvy people. You should have solid accurate information presented in a calm deliberate manner.

When I was in the executive search business, one of my candidates was close to getting an offer from one of my client companies. When I spoke to the manager of the company by phone, he informed me he was going to make an offer to another candidate. I then asked him to tell me a bit about the person. In the course of that discussion I learned that he had been employed with his current company for ten years, immediately sending up a red flag in my mind. So I asked him if we could meet before he extended the offer to discuss the matter. Since we had a great rapport and trust in each other, he agreed.

When we met I informed him of my experience with people who have been with their companies for a long time, saying to him,

"John, all of my experiences with long term people have been frustrating because yes, they accepted the offer, then when was time for them to start they backed out; for them to leave a company they're so familiar and comfortable with takes a tremendous amount of courage, especially if their manager takes them to lunch gives them pat on the back and a token raise. The chances of him rescinding before the start date are at least ninety percent, I've had it happen to me several times with candidates we represented and we got burned. Then John, we are going to lose my candidate as well and we'll have to start from scratch. My man wants the job, and he *will* start."

My sincere plea was successful and my candidate received the offer and did start the job. Presented this way, it is far from the typical scare tactic, it's sincerity, based in reality. I owed my client my insight because I knew in my heart he would get hurt with his first pick, just as I had many times. I merely painted a realistic picture of a gain with choosing my candidate and a loss with the other person. One of the best examples of communicating what's in someone's best interest and potential loss was an interview I watched on the Charlie Rose show with guest Tom Friedman,[3] the New York Times columnist and author.

The interview was a discussion about his new book, *Hot, Flat, and Crowded: Why We Need a Green Revolution—and How it Can Renew America*. The word "flat" symbolizing how we need to run faster merely to stay in place because of the explosion of wealth in the world's two most populated countries, India and China. They were discussing Friedman's travels in researching his book. He spoke of going to China, dialoging with them about investing in clean energy technology, obviously because their cooperation is vital in alleviating the environmental crisis our planet faces.

Friedman talks to Charlie about China's feelings toward their effort in developing clean energy and their attitude towards America's environmental responsibility. He relates them saying to him,

"You got to go dirty for 150 years, you Americans, now it's our turn."

He responds, "Alright guys, maybe it's your turn, take your time. Go as dirty as you want; we just need five years to invent all the clean power technology that we're going to need, as you choke to death, that you're going to want to buy. And then we're going to own the energy technology and we're going to come here and sell them to you, and we're going to clean your clock in the next great global industry. Boy, when you say that to them, that's when you see the headsets adjusting...the interpreter saying, 'What does he mean, clean your clock'? And it takes them about one minute to get it."

Friedman goes on,

"You know, I can understand how they feel. They feel you Americans ate the hors d'oeuvres, you ate the entrée, you ate the desert and you invite us for tea and coffee, then say, let's split the bill." Friedman responds to them, "You can do one of two things. You can say, you got to go dirty, so we're going to go dirty; pollute your rivers, destroy your land, make your people sick, and foul your air, or, you can say, you know what, in a world that's hot, flat, and crowded, this is going to be the next great global industry, and we're going to lead it; not America."

His dialogue makes a compelling case. One, I'm sure, that will have China thinking really hard about the direction they want to go. He brilliantly laid out both what's in their best interests, and a potential stupendous loss in both their physical welfare and pocketbook.

**Humor:** An area that should also be explored is humor, because it's probably the most effective means of dropping defenses, having the ability to render minds more flexible, receptive and open. The late great Victor Borge said,

> Laughter is the shortest distance between two people.

Humor is the antithesis of rigid thinking, helping us view situations from different perspectives, similar to a long hike through rough terrain, and then coming upon an oasis of shade, water and rest, that regenerates the body and spirit to move forward; laughter can be that oasis which rejuvenates us through the continuing stresses of life.

Humor and laughter connects the chasms of background differences, age, and agendas. When societal rules constrain our room to navigate, humor comes to the rescue by relaxing those rules and introduces mental flexibility, balance, humanness and openness into the equation. Its power lies in the fact that the brief moments of laughter have lasting effects, connecting us throughout the communication process; therefore, laughter is worth inducing before your effort toward cooperation, during, or both.

Try not to fear the impulse to be humorous, to be spontaneous and inject the good medicine of laughter. One of the funniest lines I ever heard from the sales arena was from an insurance salesman. The prospect he was talking to told him the amount of protective insurance he had for his family, which wasn't nearly enough.

He said, "You don't plan to be dead very long." Nothing gets you out of a tight situation like humor. When the famous comedian, Jonathan Winters was stopped by a police officer for speeding, the officer said to him as he approached Winters' car,

"Ok, where's the fire?"

And Winters, as only he can do, said in an effeminate tone, "In your eyes officer, in your eyes."

I'm not advocating you start becoming a comedian, however, it's something to keep in mind when beginning to present your case and can definitely stack the odds in your favor. There is a magic about laughter that can turn a mind and disarm even a hostile attitude. I once worked for a man named Roy who related a story to me about when he was out in the field selling and was continuously calling on a particular prospect, most likely going there a bit too often to win business, where the man became agitated and started shouting his displeasures at him.

In fact he went into a tirade saying something to the effect he would never do business with him if he were the last provider on the planet, even cursing at him. Rather than becoming angry and defensive, Roy simply stood there and calmly asked, "Other than that, is there any reason we couldn't do business?" The man was completely disarmed, almost immobilized trying to process the audacious question he had just heard, then broke out laughing, waved to him to come in and said get in here you so-and-so. From then on he became a good client.

Humor changes how we feel. It's difficult to experience humor and feel anger or anxiousness. Psychological studies show that humor relaxes a person and renders his mind more flexible, thereby making him more receptive to your message. Humor makes a person feel good and therefore he won't think that carefully about the proposition, and also distracts him from thinking about counter-arguments.[4] So starting off with some laughter is an excellent primer for a successful meeting and winning compliance.

Many companies have now recognized the value humor can play in strengthening the rapport of its employees, enhancing creativity, reducing stress, defusing conflict, improving communications and improving training, thereby increasing production. Dr. John Morreall was a philosophy professor whose business is now conducting seminars on the values of humor. His clients are companies such as IBM, Kodak, Xerox, and even the IRS. He's written the book, *Humor Works*. In it, he relates that when you utilize humor,

> You have created an atmosphere of consensus.

Exactly what we're looking for. His website informs us that his hobbies are plumbing and finding the remote. Mine are the study of drywall, and lint.

Humor has such a profound effect on the body and mind, it's being used in some hospitals as a means of enhancing the healing process by creating "Humor Rooms," "Lively Rooms" and "Chuckle Rooms." Laughter provides exercise by increasing the heart rate and oxygenation of the blood, where its been calculated that one-hundred laughs are equivalent to ten minutes on a rowing machine. It reduces pain by the firing of endorphins into the bloodstream, and reduces stress by lowering the levels of cortisol.

Humor also stimulates the immune system by increasing the interferon-gamma hormone that battles viruses and stimulates mental function by raising levels of adrenaline and other chemicals that prepare the body for action, therefore, I will now administer a small dose of healing medicine to you by telling one of the funniest stories I've ever heard.

A Texan stopped at a local restaurant following a day roaming around in Mexico. While sipping his Tequila, he noticed a sizzling, scrumptious looking platter being served at the next table. Not only did it look good, the smell was wonderful. He asked the waiter,

"What is that you just served?"

The waiter replied, Ah senor, you have excellent taste! Those are called Cojones de Toro, bull's testicles from de bull fight dees morning. A delicacy."

The cowboy said, "What the heck, bring me an order."

The waiter replied, "I'm so sorry senor, there is only one serving a day because there is only one bull fight each morning. If you come early and place your order, we will be sure to save you dees delicacy."

The next morning, the cowboy returned, placed his order, and that evening was served the one and only special delicacy of the day. After a few bites, inspecting his platter, he called to the waiter and said,

"These are delicious, but they're much, much smaller than the ones I saw you serve yesterday.

The waiter shrugged his shoulders and replied, "Ah, si senor...sometimes de bull wins."

**Encouraging another to listen**: From the start, a person will listen far more intently if you relate the benefit *he* will receive from your idea, before you start bouncing your idea off him. Then as you explain the concept of the idea, make it about him as much as possible. As Benjamin Disraelli said, "If you talk to people about themselves, they'll listen for hours."

After we have articulated our ideas with great eloquence, many may feel the job is about completed, however, to complete the circuit of acceptance, and then getting cooperation, we must go beyond that. When a person is listening to us, he doesn't have to think very much. In most cases, people listen passively, not purposefully, because purposeful thinking is work, so the question here becomes, how do we get people to think purposefully about our idea or ideas? Activating their thinking does it. The wonderful instrument for the ignition of activating a person's thinking is *questions.*

So far we've covered questions as a mechanism to vent feelings and derive information, however, they have multiple purposes. The question is an extraordinary conversational mechanism. Questions, coupled with skilled listening, are peering into another's mind. As if that were not enough power, he who asks the questions controls the conversation and, when asking questions, you are the center of that person's attention. Questions, as you well know, are one of the most potent tools a trial attorney utilizes to direct his witness in any direction she chooses. That is a great part of their power, directing a person's mind.

The question then, moves an individual from passive listening to dynamic active thinking, and when that question is pertinent to the idea you've just expressed, his or her mind is working on your idea, driving it home. It continues to drive it home when they have to then translate their thoughts into verbalizing an answer.

As an example, you ask, "What would be your analysis of my idea?"

Or, "What advantages do you think my idea will have?" The question completes the circuit.

Questions have a plasticity about them that can result in opposite answers from seemingly the same question, depending on how you ask it, and is why we must be cautious about the results of poles that are conducted to measure the pulse of the public; because usually we don't know how the question was asked.

A perfect story to illustrate this is a one about two priests who were arguing about whether it's proper to pray and smoke at the same time, so they decide that they would both write to the Pope to settle the dispute. About a month later after receiving their replies, they met to compare letters, where each of them insisted the Pope agreed with his position and accused the other of falsifying the answer he received from the Vatican.

Then finally one asked, "How did you express your question?"

The other priest said, "I asked whether it was proper to smoke while praying?

The Pope answered, 'Of course not, praying is too pious an activity to permit such frivolousness.'

How did you express your question?"

The priest replied, "I merely asked if it was proper to pray while smoking, and the Pope wrote, 'Of course, prayer is always good."

Questions are almost a slight-of-hand. The questioner is seemingly dependent on asking for information, where the speaker, the person being asked, senses a feeling of authority. In actuality, the questioner is commanding the other person's mind, diverting it in the direction he wants, and causing that mind to think the thoughts he chooses. Speaking to a person can or cannot be mind stimulating to that person; however, a question is immediately mind stimulating by putting his mind in gear.

The process of converting his thoughts into words clarifies them and holds them up to the light, exposing any flaws, keeping him honest. And we must always keep in mind that a person's interest is never so piqued as when he or she is speaking as, no one has ever rendered themselves bored with his or her own voice. You can see by now we've transferred a large workload over to our conversational partner through listening, questioning, then, listening again.

**Their beloved name:** Using peoples' names lights up their minds; always grabbing their attention. Using it in the course of conversation brings you emotionally closer to that individual, especially if you use it with a tone of voice that is warm and caring. Your tone of voice carrying with it far more meaning than words, it is the music behind the words. Except for savvy people, and some sales professionals, most people do not use a person's name throughout the course of conversation. We use it because this solitary technique of name use carries great emotional impact. It may seem simple and obvious, yet ironically few people practice it.

Our names are music to our ears, and hearing them makes us more apt to be influenced by the person speaking to us, and vise versa. When someone speaks to me without ever using my name during the conversation, I feel they're talking at me rather than to

*[handwritten margin notes: "Using the consultants name encouraged interaction + he became more attentive"]*

me. It must become second nature to you. I cannot talk to someone for more than a minute or two without asking what his name is because I feel uncomfortable speaking to him without using it. It is of paramount importance when trying to influence someone, and get someone to listen to you, to use his beloved name in your discourse, using it with warmth, and even a smile.

**Pearly whites:** A smile is an emotional reward to the person you're sending the smile to, and more importantly *it drops defenses!* It's disarming. Stanford researchers Turhan Canli and John Gabrielli attached a functional magnetic resonance imaging scanner (fMRI) to participants in order to read their brains' response to facial expressions. The scanner focused on the amygdala, a pea-sized area of the brain associated with emotion and memory found directly behind the eyes. The participants looked at pictures of faces depicting a variety of expressions and when these subjects looked at happy faces, the amygdala "lit-up", especially in those participants who had extrovert personalities.[5]

The vision of a smile had an immediate and direct impact on the brain. Therefore, you have the power to light-up a person's mind, by giving her a generous smile along with the sound of her name— you're now communicating directly to her emotional center, which as you remember, is the part of us that makes the final decision.

**Touch:** It's no secret that if a person *feels* closer to you, she'll listen more closely. One profound element in human connection is touch. In his book, *Touching: The Human Significance of the Skin,* the late renowned anthropologist Ashley Montagu relates this,

Although touch is not itself an emotion, its sensory elements induce those neural, glandular, muscular, and mental changes which in combination we call emotion. Hence touch is not experienced as a simple physical modality, as sensation, but affectively, as emotion.

We in America generally do not touch each other much, there seems to be an unwritten taboo. Touching someone appropriately, however, is an excellent way to his or her heart, it speaks to us on the deepest level of our humanness. Yes, in our modern ultra-sensitive society, you must be cautious about touch, especially in the workplace. Yet, we *do* feel closer and have a stronger connection, to anyone we touch, or likewise, when *we* are touched in an appropriate manner.

Other than the handshake, another appropriate place to lightly touch anyone is the outside part of the forearm when talking to him or her. It's accepted, especially at the moment when you're making a conversational point, or asking an exciting question as in,

"Do you know who got a promotion?"
or, "Guess who's pregnant?"

To those people we are close to, we have the freedom to use touch any time we wish and as often as we wish. Using touch with them will significantly enhance communication and profoundly impact understanding, a sense of caring, and intimacy.

Touch conveys warmth, togetherness, acceptance, tenderness and a sincere desire to communicate, therefore, a light touch when asking someone to listen to us can go a long way to how well he or she listens to us. It's a small thing with a large psychological and emotional impact. Dr. Montagu says,

> The language of the senses, in which all of us can be socialized, is capable of enlarging our appreciation and of deepening our understanding of each other and the world in which we live. Chief among these languages is touching. The communications we transmit through touch constitute the most powerful means of establishing human relationships, the foundation of experience.

All these techniques used collectively form a synergy in bringing a person to listen on both an emotional and intellectual level, giving you much greater odds in him or her cooperating.

**Coming to Agreement:** In the sales world there is a term called *closing*. Basically it means to get a commitment. There are numerous techniques of closing in trying to bring a potential customer to a decision, something we all tend to avoid. The one close, my favorite, is called the *order blank close*. What's great about it is its simplicity. It simply means, ask for the order. It's also one of the most difficult for many people probably because of its directness, promoting an irrational fear within the person who needs to ask. The overriding fear is driven by the *fear of rejection*. This fear is so pervasive, that people will do almost anything to avoid it.

In thinking of entering a career in sales, it's the number one fear, and, when a man wants to approach a woman he's interested in, the fear of rejection is overwhelming because it threatens the very essence of his manhood. The only way to overcome this fear is to practice asking for what you're after. The fear, as I guess most fears are, is over-exaggerated; the Earth will not open and swallow you and nothing is going to blow up in your face. I'm sure you've heard the phrase, *ask for what you want*. That's exactly what the order blank close is and you'd be surprised at what you can get when you do. It's a matter of having some common sense logic as to know when to ask.

In the process of enlisting the cooperation of another person, there is a point at which it's appropriate to ask for a commitment to your idea, unless, of course, she voluntarily pronounces she's all for it. Don't fear a hesitation on her part, or even a "no." If you get that response, it informs you of your progress so far, meaning you have more work to do...starting with questions to perhaps draw her out or backing off for awhile, abandoning pressure and become neutral, and trying again later. I remember a line from Og Mandingo's book, *The Greatest Salesman in the World*,

> No longer will I judge a man on one meeting; no longer will I fail to call again tomorrow on he who meets me with hate today. This day he will not buy gold chariots for a penny, yet tomorrow he would exchange his home for a tree.

When you do get a yes, a commitment, it's vital *you do not buy it back*. Once they verbalize an agreement move on from there...it's done. You have closed; don't unclose. Your discourse from there forward is executing the idea, not giving the other person a dubious sense that there is still a question about her decision. If you subtly communicate that impression, more times than not people will gravitate toward changing their minds, because you've given them the feeling they have the option. They told you "yes"; take it to the bank.

**Reciprocity on steroids:** We've discussed the use of the *Employee or Member Dossier* and how it utilizes the rule of reciprocity. Here we're going to explore it a bit further as a technique you may want to use, when appropriate. At one time I attended marshal arts classes. This particular marshal art is called *aikido*. In aikido there are no strikes or staccato moves, rather a flowing graceful engagement, a physically sophisticated art of harmonizing with the other person's energy to your advantage and most of the moves consist of throwing the opponent, so when practicing aikido one must learn how to fall.

It's beautiful and fascinating to watch, and to learn. This reciprocity technique employs the same concept whereby you "go with" the resistance of the other person, much the same as using assurance phrases we covered earlier.

The difference with this technique is that you are psychologically priming the person for the reciprocity response before you deliver it. That is, when you ask for whatever cooperation you want, you ask for much more than what you actually want, where the person is almost certain to say, "no." When the negative response is expressed, you merely concede to it—harmonizing with their inclination, "I understand."

Now, right at this juncture is the power because the concession you made is something you've "given" to that person. Emotionally, they interpret this as actually receiving something from you; then, you can ask for what you really want any time after that. It could be right then, or it could be later, whenever you choose. When the time comes to make your request, which will be much less than what you originally asked for, the person will now feel the reciprocity response to reciprocate, and be emotionally driven to agree to it, to fulfill his perceived "obligation" to you.

What makes this technique even more compelling is that it automatically incorporates another psychological response mechanism—the method of *sequential requests*. There are two items; one is in stark contrast to the other. If we are presented with one *or* the other, we experience them as they are, without comparison, however, if we are presented with them in sequence, one after the other; the second one is experienced much differently. As an example, if I ask you to lend me fifty-dollars and you say no, I accept your response, and then ask you for twenty-dollars, you will perceive the twenty-dollars as much less than if I asked you for it first; therefore you are much more likely to agree to grease me.

Or, let's say we worked at the same company and I came to you and asked if you would help me finish a project by the end of day, requiring three hours of your time, and you politely refuse. Again, I politely accept it, then I ask you if you could complete just one file for me. That one file will seem much more palatable than if I requested it of you first. So, the rule of reciprocity used this way amplifies its power to attain agreement through the reciprocity principle itself, and, through comparative impression.

**The Power of Personal Letters:** Through letters, the power of the written word, we can be especially effective in the pursuit of cooperation as another arrow in your quiver of communicative options. Receiving a personal letter, whether hand written or typed, is an intimate way to communicate and something you may want to consider in emotionally reaching people.

With the tactile sensation of being held in the hands while thoughts emanate from the page, the reader feels a powerful sense of your presence, evoking a special feeling, an extra something that someone has extended themselves to you in the time invested to create it—they feel they are important. The personal written word has its own magic of communication and conveys a deliberation and profoundness that reaches a deeper level, especially in our hectic, impersonal and speed driven technological society of cell phones, emails, text messaging, faxes and phone-mail. A personal letter stands alone in communicating at a profound level. No modern gadget can replace a letter. It can be more intimate than a conversation, and go so far as to be called a gift.

Yet, it seems to have become a lost art. *The great advantage of a letter is that it gives the other person time to process her feelings without the pressure of having to reply immediately.* Because of its intimacy, we may be reluctant to use the medium of letters; on the other hand, that *is* its power. Since writing a letter brings forth deeper thoughts, we may fear exposing too much of ourselves, making us feel vulnerable. In the business environment its use is normal; in the social environment its use is rare, and because of that, it carries great impact.

When you write, your thoughts are formed differently than when you verbalize them, and therefore allow you to communicate utilizing a different part of your brain. As you write, it's common for new insights to form and it offers a valuable complement to your verbal communication. It is certainly a departure from our fast paced life style, slowing you down, quieting the mind, focusing the mind and activating the creative process, when at times, thoughts will bubble up that surprise you, bringing with them a new understanding and a different perspective.

Writing helps us to better communicate because it promotes mental clarity and more accurate reasoning. Writing resists expressing fuzzy thoughts because it's staring right back at you and if it makes little sense, you're forced to reformulate, sharpening your thinking and aiding you greatly in articulating your ideas and feelings more accurately than when verbalizing them. The only important rules to follow are to state your case, express yourself, be honest, be respectful, be sensitive, be complimentary and have it come from the heart.

When you then speak with that person, your conversation will begin at a deeper level, further enhancing your communication. It is the art of staying connected. Another great advantage of writing a letter is that it can be read over and over again. The three ways to send a personal letter are, handwritten, computer generated printed document with a few sentences in your own handwriting or computer generated only.

I'm not including letters by email here because they lack the physical nature of words on paper, although they could suffice if you have to use them. One evening I heard Andy Rooney lament that it's sad we hardly ever get a letter from a friend or relative in the mail any more, and that emails are about as charming as a freight-train. They will, though, serve your purpose when speed is of the essence, nevertheless, the physicality of receiving an envelope and the pleasurable excitement in anticipation of opening it, along with the visual aesthetics and tactile sensation of holding it is unmatched by pixels on a screen.

Handwritten, of course, is much more intimate, carrying with it the message of how important the recipient is to you. When requesting cooperation through a letter, it allows the person the luxury to relax and mull it over, rather than feeling the discomfort of responding immediately. As in any good letter, be succinct and to the point; be direct, ask for what you want; express gratitude for their help and close with warmth.

It will be well worth your effort to at least try this timeless art form of communication. You will be unique in doing so.

## Assertiveness

At this point it would be prudent to rate yourself as to where you fall on a behavior continuum, so you have a point from which to work toward better communication and rapport.

There are four basic communication styles. The first is aggressive. This is where people feel their rights are predominant over all others and are ego-based, always wanting to be listened to; their needs are to be gratified, without any reciprocation toward other people being heard or having their needs being met. This is accomplished by being overbearing, intimidating, or through manipulation such as gratuitous praise, nagging and giving unwanted advise.

Second is the passive personality. Of course it's the opposite of being aggressive. These people rarely expose or espouse what they think or feel and behave in ways suggesting the other person's needs, is more important than their own needs. Seldom do they participate or interact with people voluntarily. They tend to be subservient to the wishes of others and seldom assert their own.

Third, there is passive-aggressive. This communication type won't express anything towards having their needs met and nor will they acknowledge the needs of others. They usually won't do what they've agreed to do, where failing to deliver is their way of communicating that their needs are not met. Where there is disagreement, the passive aggressive expresses his anger indirectly, which results in exacerbating conflict rather than working towards a solution.

Fourth, is assertive. Assertive people can communicate their feelings and needs and are also sensitive to the needs of others. Not only will they express their needs and wants, they are happy to state why, being open to discussing an arrangement that is gratifying to both parties.

Between these four personality types, it doesn't take a psychoanalyst to determine which is the healthiest, most effective and most competent—it is of course assertiveness. Being assertive is merely being honest when you communicate with others, honoring yourself and other people. Yes, when being honest, it sometimes requires courage in expressing yourself, and that's why it's efficient at building self-esteem. Many of the techniques presented in this book will be instrumental in maintaining the balance between aggressiveness and passivity and toward assertiveness.

For instance, the order blank close we covered earlier is an excellent example. It simply states, "Ask for what you want." This is assertiveness at its finest. It's straightforward, honest and calm. Simply express

*I feel I have an assertive communication style able to*

your desire. This is an important component of being assertive and living your life more dynamically.

In a wonderful magazine article addressing this issue, the author describes her conversation with a girlfriend who sadly states that she wants her husband to have more sex with her. The author then asks her if she has told him how she feels? Fearing that she would come across as a nag or being dissatisfied, she states that she could never bring herself to tell him. Then this woman says she doesn't necessarily want to have more sex…that she just wants him to want her to have more sex. She does but she doesn't. Contradictory? Yes! The author points out that it would be much less costly emotionally if she were to face him and state simply what she wants, rather than continually suppress those wants.

A second acquaintance of hers, a man, relates that his wife constantly attacks him verbally, to the point that he fears he'll have to end his marriage. She asks him, "Why don't you tell her?" Because he fears he'll come across as weak if he does and that it would be humiliating. He can't bring himself to express what he wants. She ends the article with these words: "You can. You must." These two stories perfectly illustrate the folly we inflict on ourselves when we disrespect what we want to the point of suppression and depression. There's no easy way to do it other than take a deep breath and express what you want…what you feel from within.

Learning how to say "no," is another excellent way to practice asserting yourself. It's not new; likely, you've heard this before; nevertheless it's important. If you're doing something merely to make another person happy while violating your own rights, that's the time to

*communicate effectively in any given situation*

exercise the utterance of "no." This is not to be confused with selfishness, where doing only what you want is what counts. It's all a matter of balance. Rely on your own best judgment and what feels right, keeping in the back of your mind that there is an appropriate time to say no.

Some may feel that declining a request is unkind, that they are inflicting pain upon the person who's asking. It's understandable and normal; we all feel it. Yet unkind cuts both ways. When you honor only the other person's wishes, you are being unkind to yourself, therefore, when you develop honoring yourself, you then have permission to be kind to yourself. It's quite all right to say, "I don't want to go," or "I don't feel up to doing that," or, "I'm tired of carrying that burden."

Further, fight the need to over-explain or defend your decision. Just be honest and graceful. You'll find it liberating. Remember there is a large difference in possibly disappointing someone with a "no" answer, and the feeling that you'll hurt them beyond repair, or that they'll despise you because you've declined. Ken Keyes, author of *Handbook to Higher Consciousness,* enlightens us with,

> When you resent helping someone, this creates obligations, duality, and separation. You cannot psychologically afford to give such help, and the recipient cannot afford to receive it. The price in personal distance and separation is too high if you give to avoid a feeling of "guilt" or from a "should" or "ought" motivation.

I get together with about ten of my old school buddies once a month for lunch or drinks. I've noticed that in our group, three of them will not utter a single opinion about any of the many subjects at hand as we solve the world's problems; one of them though is all too glad to offer his omniscient view in an overbearing manner. I call him the High Lama. It's interesting to watch the contrast between the two types.

If you recognize yourself as a person that's somewhat overbearing, demanding or manipulative, developing your listening skills will be of enormous benefit as will the next chapter dealing with ego. Assertiveness is a learned skill and is more a way of being than it is a personality type.

## Surrendering Our People Skills through Modern Technology

Our brains are being conditioned, evolving away from fundamental social and communication skills. This conditioning is coming from massive amounts of time being spent with the Internet, computer games, television, Blackberry, phone-mail and email, where we are plugged-in and tuned-out; averting direct human contact. If you're in sales, you probably have been aware of this trend for a while now, experiencing how difficult it is to communicate with a prospect and even your clients, where even the secretaries are on phone-mail.

Who among us is not excruciatingly exasperated when we attempt to call a company, only to be greeted with the maddening litany of press 1, press 2, press 3, where each press brings another menu of options—all I want to do is communicate with a human-being! It seems no one wants to verbally communicate—an ongoing pursuit of social isolation—no talking allowed. This movement toward the technological and away from social human interaction, according to scientists, is atrophying the brain's neural circuitry that controls our skill level with people, especially in young people whose minds are much more malleable.

According to a study by the Kaiser Family Foundation, in collaboration with researchers from Stanford University, eight to eighteen year-olds devote more than 53 hours a week to entertainment media (TV, video games and computers). There are times when the bits and bytes of technology become peoples' only reality. One incident I experienced was when I worked in downtown Chicago, where I parked in a garage that utilized a monthly prepaid computer card that had to be inserted into a machine when you entered and again when you left in order to open the gate.

Being is sales, it wasn't unusual to leave the lot and reenter several times a day. One afternoon, I came back to the garage, inserted my card into the machine and the gate didn't rise so I could enter. I went into the office and informed the garage manager. We both went back to the gate area and he tried the card himself; again it didn't work. He then said he would go back to the office and check the card with the in-and-out log from the main computer, or something of that nature. After a few moments he came back and uttered an unbelievable statement to me.

There I was standing behind the gate with a two-ton car idling behind me; he, holding my card in his hand, and looking me straight in the eye, said these unforgettable words,

"You didn't leave."

As I stood there in dumbfounded awe, I could picture Rod Serling stepping out of the shadows saying,

> Picture if you will, a man, a car, a parking lot, on one sunny afternoon, when Joe, a hard-working salesman who lives a typically normal life in a relaxed suburb of Chicago, drove into...*The Twilight Zone.*

The manager didn't say there must be a glitch in the card or computer, no, that would have required reflective thought.

When the reality on the computer screen overrides the "other" reality of life, then it becomes a bit dangerous. Unfortunately, this is not an isolated case. We've all experienced trying to tell people on the other end of the line what the truth is, yet, their computer screen is their god representing all of reality, and when you speak to them, and then to their managers, and they all tell you there's nothing they can do, you can't help but wonder, who's in control? Are we telling the computers what to do, or are they telling us?

Extreme immersion into technology like the Internet is a distraction from our humanity and will move us toward an ever-increasing divide in our close relationships, as well as effective communication with our fellow humans.

Some medical and scientific researchers believe that too much technological stimulation compromises the imagination by limiting your interactions to people that only share your point of view. Staring at a computer screen isn't conducive to a diversity of experiences that can spark imagination and give birth to new ideas. Face-to-face communication *along with* technological communication empowers us in maintaining and enhancing our creative juices.

Rather than email, we can call and speak to that person, becoming more expertise in our listening skills;

rather than call, we can meet and converse eyeball to eyeball, sharpening our skills to perceive facial expressions, body language, and "tells". Making a conscious effort to balance the technology time with quality human interpersonal time will keep us proficient in all of modern life.

# Ego and Competence

*Enlightenment is your ego's greatest disappointment.*
—Swami Muktananda

*There is no end to the nonsense that the
rational mind can spin out as the pawn of the ego.*
—Ken Keyes

*If you're intelligent, you'll agree with me.*
—Humble acquaintance

*Ego is not your Amigo*
—Taylor Haskins


It is estimated that ego costs companies 6 to 15 percent of annual revenue. Even if it accounts for only 6 percent of revenue, the annual cost of ego would translate to nearly $1.1 billion to the average Fortune 500 company or roughly equal to the average annual profit of these same companies.[1] Excessive ego will make you do strange things, including committing career-suicide.

An article in *Fortune* magazine related the following:

> An excess of ego can make you promise more than you can deliver, fly too high, ignore other people. Abundant self-regard is an affliction that killed many a corporate career. It can make a CEO deaf: Think Doug Ivester tuning out his lieutenants and his board of directors at Coke. And blind: Think Lucent's Rich McGinn, oblivious to the signs of his ouster until the very end. And dumb: Think Mattel's Jill Barad. A few years ago Barad exhorted her staff to create a "CEO Barbie" even as Mattel's sales and marketing people argued that most little girls don't know what a CEO is. Barad insisted that the doll wear a pink Chanel

suit with gold buttons just like hers and be accessorized with a bumblebee pin like the one she always wore. CEO Barbie got the boot. So did Barad.[2]

We have the egos of Kenneth Lay, a PhD economist, and Jeffrey Skilling, both top officers of Enron, who out of sheer ego-greed, brought the company to its demise losing $50 billion of market capitol in ten months, and ruining the financial lives of hundreds of employee stockholders. They cooked the books and surreptitiously sold their stock, while encouraging their employees to retain theirs. There is Bernard Ebbers of WorldCom convicted on nine counts of accounting fraud to the tune of $11 billion leading to the largest bankruptcy in U.S. history in 2005.

Then there is Dennis Kozlowski, CEO of Tyco, found guilty of stealing $120 million, convicted of grand larceny and conspiracy. Another, Richard Scrushy, founder of HealthSouth, a global health care company, accused of directing a $2.7 billion accounting fraud, then convicted of bribery and mail fraud. All of them, brilliant, epically successful men whose egos were flying close to the Sun, derailing their businesses and brought to an end, lavishly opulent personal lives most of us can only dream about.

Then there is the $50 billion Ponzi king, Bernie Madoff, who perpetrated the biggest scam in history. He had a Midas Touch reputation for producing high investment returns, and people clamored to give him their money. So blatantly arrogant, Madoff sent out bogus portfolio reports to his investors of stocks he never invested in, ultimately bringing them to financial ruin. Reportedly, this is a man who made about $25,000,000 a year legally, and could have sold his business for a billion dollars. He will spend the rest of his life in prison.

If it were not for Madoff, Marc Dreier would probably have held the dubious title as the most famous white-collar criminal in America. His Ponzi scheme was overshadowed by Madoff's arrest just after Dreier was exposed. Marc Dreier was a highly respected attorney with a large Park Avenue law firm. He has Yale and Harvard law degrees, and was portrayed by many judges that he appeared in front of, as probably the best attorney they'd ever seen. Dreier bilked $400 million from dozens of investment firms over a four-year period and is now serving a twenty-year prison term. In an interview he said,

"I had an ambition that I needed to feed,"
and also stated,

"I wanted to be as important as I thought I was; deserved to be."

His ego sabotaged his greatness.

Three U.S. automobile manufacturers were on the precipice of bankruptcy, when our government decided to bail them out with loans. These are the executives who, rather than innovate their vehicles in a new direction as oil prices began to inflate, decided to subsidize gasoline if we purchased gas hogs like the Hummer or a Suburban from them. They refused to acknowledge, let alone act upon, the new and obviously crucial information about where their market was heading.

Business, however, is only one facet of life where ego plays havoc with competence. There's family life, friendships, government, religion, and education; all vulnerable to gross dysfunction fueled by egos. Even the bonds of romance won't be able to survive an ego that places its needs above that of the relationship. One good definition of ego I've found is *a fear based and unnatural aberration of mind, which arises to protect personal integrity.* It implies that our ego was originally created to serve a positive purpose, perhaps for self-protection in a dangerous world.

Renowned psychotherapist, Nathaniel Branden, states that,

> Egoism holds that man is an end in himself; altruism holds that man is a means to the ends of others. Egoism holds that, morally, the beneficiary of an action should be the person who acts; altruism holds that, morally, the beneficiary of an action should be someone *other* that the person who acts.[3]

It seems to me that between the two, being at opposite sides of the spectrum, they should come together in balance if we are to be our most competent selves. It's when one of these becomes weighted to the extent of impeding optimum decision making ability and weakens skills relating to human relations, that it diminishes successful functionality.

The ego, similar to bureaucracy, at some point can grow into a bloated self-serving entity that serves mostly to protect itself and its survival, becoming increasingly incompetent to the functional purpose for which it was first created. At that point, a person's ego is enlarged to the extent of being paranoid, all too ready to be offended and results in over-protecting itself from anything that would deflate it, including truth and reality. When that happens competency is compromised, weakening a person's effectiveness, especially in the area of people skills—human interaction. Competency then, is inversely proportional to the size of the ego.

An individual in a position of power can certainly control the people subordinate to her. She can control, to a large extent, their time, where they go, how they direct their efforts and what they can and cannot do. If she is enslaved by an over-demanding ego, she could also use intimidation to get temporary results, and intimidation is emblematic of incompetence. But, to enlist peoples' minds, hearts, and spirit, thereby capturing the enormous energy attendant with it, demands skill.

The founder of analytical psychiatry and celebrated Swiss psychiatrist, Carl Jung, enlightens us with,

> An inflated consciousness is always egocentric and conscious of nothing but its own existence. It is incapable of learning from the past, incapable of understanding contemporary events, and incapable of drawing right conclusions about the future. It is hypnotized by itself and therefore cannot be argued with. It inevitably dooms itself to calamities that must strike it dead.

The ego, along with all of the self-protection and its constant alertness for potential threats, expends an enormous amount of emotional and psychic energy that can otherwise be used for far more constructive endeavors. Deepak Chopra writes,

> An ego need can be defined as anything that bolsters "me."

and,

> We have all been conditioned to obey ego needs blindly.[4]

My own description of an ego that is indulged is one that is uninterested in empathy, only in stroking itself; lacking the ability to read other peoples' emotions, preoccupied only in its own nurturing; is uninterested in listening, but captive to its own internal dialogue and can hear nothing else; it lacks the sensitivity of another's needs and distress, only what's in its own benefit; and is uninterested in cooperation, only concerned with control through manipulation. Understanding is abhorrent to the ego. Ego feels strong and invincible, but in fact is weak because it continually grovels for things from the outside to prop itself up.

The challenge for all of us is to get off and stay off this path, challenging because the ego is insidious and seductive, and never gets enough. Taming the ego necessarily renders us more proficient in our inter-relationships with people, rendering us more competent because now the focus is off ourselves, and onto the people in our lives. The energy can now be diverted toward a sincere quest in developing fine-honed people skills. Ambrose Bierce, the late American journalist, offers this humorous statement about ego,

"Egotist: a person of low taste, more interested in himself than in me."

In his superb book, *Wealth Addiction,* Philip Slater states this about the ego,

> Egos like to restrict and control information. Every organism has an information system that doesn't involve the Ego, but from the Ego's point of view it is too loose, too flexible, too spontaneous, too democratic. The Ego likes to streamline and simplify this system and redesign it on a binary basis. Only 'relevant' information gets to the palace at all—the

rest is ignored. Despots hate negative feedback, because it always includes the message that they are arrogating too much power to themselves, creating a top-heavy over centralized structure with an ever-narrowing power base—a message they obviously don't want to hear. We call this shutting off critical information 'repression,' whether it occurs at the political level or the psychological level.

This articulate representation of the ego clearly shows that an out-of-control ego necessarily moves an individual toward incompetence. The overriding reason being that the ego filters out reality in favor of the reality of the mind of that individual, allowing only the information it wants to hear, and nothing more. Less information, or perhaps even worse, half-truths, renders us less competent. Slater goes on to say,

> Since the Ego likes to see itself as a lonely captain at the helm of a beleaguered ship of state, it tries to pass off any malfunctions in the organism as the result not of the Ego's own authoritarian and over centralized rule, but of "outside agitators."

Although we cannot rid ourselves entirely of our egos because it permeates through the conscious and into the subconscious, nor would we necessarily want to, because I believe, in balance, it does serve some good purpose. Nevertheless, we can make ourselves more aware of when its defenses surface and compromise our competence. The ego is not inquisitive since it's not interested in new information that might weaken its reign. Let us take a simple example of this at work. We men have an infamous reputation for refusing to ask for directions. I don't know if it's true with most men, yet that is the perception.

When a person is obviously lost and that person insists he's not, that's the ego's first step of entrapment by putting that person into a state of denial. A good definition for denial is a blatant rejection of an obvious truth. When denial is firmly in place, the second step is to necessarily seal-off any and all conduits of information—I will not ask, I will not seek facts. Now let's think about this for a moment. We have here a person who has voluntarily turned a blind eye and deaf ear to data that could promote a more successful and efficient outcome for what he's trying to do.

In essence the message is, "I fear breaking my spellbound denial; I fear being told something I don't know and I fear leaving my own little world and being thrust into the real one." I ask you, is this not the pursuit of incompetence? This person will feel he's independent, and *that* independence is an irrational *independence from reality.* This simple example represents the same mechanism that kicks-in when we're wrestling with other more complex problems that life throws our way. When some women are looking for that special man to enter their lives, they many times find him without knowing because they cut off information precipitously, and banish him from their lives prematurely. As two clinical psychologists point out,

> Some women make these decisions with frightening speed, according to superficial and incomplete data.[5]

So, if you find yourself being resistant to new information you may not *want* to hear or are uncomfortable with, yet could be pertinent to a particular problem or situation, that's a tall red flag to relax your defenses or preconceived beliefs and to consider the information as objectively as you can. It will take practice, and mental courage. We hold dear many of our views. New information threatens that view and the threat you feel is the ego poking you in the eye...back off, get away, turn away, so you can feel comfortable again with a false sense of control.

Therefore, *less information*—and the price—less competence, whereas more information increases your options, expanding the information at hand in which to make your most competent decision. Yes, it's insidious, and none of us can readily afford it. The ego develops undesirable traits like denial and rationalization to help keep us in our comfort zone, thereby avoiding any type of anxiety. It shackles us to a sort of force field, fending us against the "foes" of *our* reality that might undermine the ego's fragility and perceived vulnerability. The problem is always *out there,* empowering what's out there to control us. We then become reactive rather than proactive, diminishing once again, our competency.

Taming the ego, then, not only helps us look at our world with more clarity, but is also liberating, preparing us to look more objectively at the world with much less fear and anxiety that it might contradict our present beliefs, and gives us a much greater appreciation for what is, rather than what we want it to be. Einstein says, "A man should look for what is, and not for what he thinks should be." That's worth the effort to develop, and be on constant vigil for. For the ego, like the frog that sees only what it could eat for its survival, honors only the selective data that supports its beliefs and discards everything else, for *its* own survival.

There is a beautifully profound Buddha story called *The Lost Son,* which exemplifies the price we pay for our intractable belief systems.

> A young widower, who loved his five-year-old son very much, was away on business when bandits came and burned down the whole village and took his son away. When the man returned, he saw the ruins and panicked. The man took the burnt corpse of an infant to be that of his son and cried uncontrollably. He organized a cremation ceremony, collected the ashes and put them in a beautiful little bag, which he always kept with him.
>
> Soon afterwards, his real son escaped from the bandits and found his way home. He arrived at his father's new cottage at midnight and knocked at the door. The father, still grieving asked, "Who is it?" The child answered, "It is me Papa, open the door!" But in his agitated state of mind, convinced his son was dead, the father thought that some young boy was making fun of him. He shouted: "Go away" and continued to cry. The child knocked again and pleaded, "Papa, it's me your son, please open the door." Still his father responded, "Go away." So, the child left. Father and son never saw each other again.

After this story, the Buddha said,

> Sometime, somewhere, you take something to be the truth. If you cling to it so much, even when the truth comes in person and knocks on your door, you will not open it.

The ego accesses the emotional part of ourselves because the emotional mind is far quicker than the rational mind. In doing so it precludes and circumvents analytical consideration. This reflexive action comes from remnants of our primitive selves, where it was a matter of survival to act quickly—the fight or flight syndrome. For any of our ancient ancestors, hesitating for an instant could very likely result in being lunch. According to psychologists, this rapid response is measured in thousandths of a second, where in our modern world, necessarily sacrifices accuracy for speed.

Our emotions provide the radar for danger, and in doing so create a drawback because we could make snap-judgments that will tend to be misguided. The ego favors quick black and white decisions because it thinks in binary terms, and paints with a broad-brush. Our rational side knows this is unrealistic, because we know that life has many shades of gray with infinite nuances. We live in a massively complex world, where life is a tangle of paradoxes. To negotiate this uncertainty, the ego automatically tries to simplify life's confusions and chaos, in a pathetic attempt to grasp certainty.

The ego looks at the world through its own grid, which it superimposes on the world, fitting all of life into neat little partitions, creating an illusion of simplicity, making it easy for us, and it, because it is lazy to boot. Everything is categorical: see where it fits, no thinking necessary. We need not put forth any effort in considering the constant flow of information we face daily and sort out facts. No mental energy needed to make hard decisions. Just throw it in the automatic response bin.

Using canoeing, where the trick is to paddle on both sides of the canoe, is an excellent analogy. That simple fact can escape us when it comes to thinking, only absorbing views that support what we already think and only expressing opinions that do the same.

Paddling just on the right, or just the left, they go in circles, rather than forward. The logical part of yourself is responsive to changing circumstances, changing facts and altered situations, where you would then act in an appropriate manner to compensate.

The ego doesn't honor change or new information; its only alliance is to its rigid doctrine that may have been appropriate a few decades ago, or that may have been conditioned into us as a child by well meaning people, educators, culture or theology. It is unchanging, unalterable and unyielding if we allow it to have its own way. We may interpret our constancy of mind with strength and character, where in fact it has become a stagnant ideology unable to adapt to reality that is constantly changing.

We may also associate changing our minds with weakness, where in fact it's our ego refusing to understand and incorporate new information into our principles that would help us perform more competently in a rapid, ever changing world. Placing our convictions in a cement foundation makes us feel secure and also feel that if we modify those beliefs to harmonize with new insights, it will destabilize our world. This is ego fear. In actuality, embracing fresh views that have intrinsic merit enhances our ability to navigate through the world far more successfully.

In the movie, *The Bridges of Madison County*, Kincaid tells Francesca, "The only thing you can count on that doesn't change, *is* change." Our ideologies should not be static, rather a process of growth and change that are consistent with reality. This doesn't mean we become gullible to every idea that's presented to us, it does means we honestly assess without bias or fear, new concepts, with an open mind, and be excited about new discovery. Looking at it in a broad context, man would never be as advanced without adaptation.

From being the naked savages we once were to a decent civilized species, rested on our ability to change how we think. Progress would never have been possible without it. Science welcomes new information with open arms, obviously because it would ossify into a belief system if it didn't. The sun would revolve around the Earth, a magician would be burned at the stake, going faster than thirty-miles an hour would dislodge our internal organs, bloodletting would be the cure for pneumonia and epilepsy would be a one-way ticket to the funny farm. Releasing old belief systems is hardly on your ego's priority list. It lusts for security, safety and "protection," and those hallowed beliefs cater to it.

I heard a lecturer suggest that a simple way to help weaken our ego's hold on us, is by performing small kindnesses to others as often as we can, even to strangers. perhaps daily. Since the ego is only concerned with itself, behaving in a way that's of concern to others would seem deleterious to its power. The effort is nothing paramount, but the intent is. Things as simple as a giving someone a smile, allowing someone in front of you at the grocery checkout counter if they have only one or two items to purchase, giving permission to go ahead in traffic, giving a couple of dollars to a homeless person, saying a kind word to someone, sincerely complimenting people more often or using peoples' names with a caring tone of voice and doing it more often, etc.

Having your antennae up for these opportunities is the power behind it, because your attitude will be substantially modified into the welfare of others, however, the ego is clever and seductive. As an example, Frederick Nietzsche says,

> He that humbleth himself wishes to be exalted.

This could easily have the opposite effect where the ego pats itself on the back inflating itself even further by saying, "What a great person I am; just look at how I'm taking the time and effort to be concerned with helping other people; I'm a good caring person. Someone…give me a plaque and a kiss."

Despite this potential danger, it's a good idea, provided you keep your intent coming from a place of trying to develop kindness and compassion. It will take close introspection as you do this, being ruthlessly honest with yourself, which is something the ego loathes. It reminds me of the beautiful words I once heard my aunt Rose DeVito say,

> Do good and forget about it.

That's about as ego-liberated as it gets.

## A Word About Kindness

A definition of kindness I like, is the behavior that is distinguished by the act of being charitable, with an authentic heartfelt empathy for others. The concept of love is used a lot. We talk of having love for our fellow man, and religion sermonizes about it. But kindness is the evidence of love, where the rubber meets the road—the bottom line.

We are all too aware of the overabundance of pain in our world, and that anytime we act with discourtesy or animosity toward another person, we simply add to it. Kindness is truly a subtractor from that aggregate pain. There are many of our fellow citizens who are operating in desperation and on the brink of a breaking point, and we, with one unkind word or gesture could topple those people off the edge, or with a kind word or act, possibly be their savior. We most likely would never know.

One of the most interesting aspects of performing an act of kindness is the production of serotonin, an endorphin that has the dual benefits of strengthening the immune system and helping to nullify depression and stress. The utterly fascinating thing is that not only does the giver of kindness have an increase of serotonin, but also does the recipient, and even those who witness the act of kindness.[6] We are not talking about major acts here. We are talking about small acts of kindness that can, if you choose, punctuate each and every day of your life where everybody wins. That's some powerful stuff.

Many studies have shown that kindness induces a heightened sense of well being, increased energy, increased longevity, weakens insomnia, promotes a stronger immune system, reduces pain, strengthens the cardiovascular system, and reduces stomach acid; a snake-oil salesman couldn't promise more. Do good and forget about it. Your body won't.

A lit known method to help you dynamically influence people is this: *allow yourself to be influenced.* I know it sounds strange, yet it is a powerful psychological tool. It's not a tool to be used manipulatively; it should be used with honesty, which is far more effective. The analysis behind the concept is this: *When you let a person know they have influenced your mind, she feels this—you have respected my thoughts enough to change your thinking. You have honored me—ironically, in return, this gift to her empowers you to be of much greater influence with her.* So be sensitive to opportunities to be influenced by someone you want to have greater influence *with*. The simple logic of this concept is that when *you* recognize and acknowledge a person's insight, how could they not be impressed with you and your intellectual admiration of their wisdom. One caveat: this does not mean becoming a yes-man.

There is a world of difference between the two. That will lose you respect. You cannot make anyone feel honored who doesn't have respect for you. When a person makes an excellent point that adds to your own knowledge, let her know she has affected your mind. It's difficult to think of anything else that can be such a wonderful compliment to any of us—*you have affected my mind.*

The reason I've included this method in this chapter rather than the previous chapter of strategies is because it speaks directly to ego. This practice helps a great deal in taming the ego because the ego abhors being influenced; its defense mechanism will do anything to protect its ideology including a refusal to understand anything that's not in clinging alliance to its own belief system no matter how irrefutable or insightful the logic is.

Another strategy to point out here because it speaks directly to ego, is handling anger in another person. This is challenging to handle because most of the time when anger is being expressed, especially when directed toward us, our defense mechanism goes on automatic pilot. This is the ego lodging a pointed branch into your anus propelling you into a programmed instantaneous reflex reaction, rather than responding. Whenever you're handling anger, take a tip from the wonderfully exquisite poet, Emily Dickinson:

> Anger as soon as fed is dead—
> Tis starving makes it fat.

These are insightful words to say the least. When someone is venting his anger toward you, allow him to do just that. Listen! Let him vent...*when fed is dead*. The normal tendency is to speak in a futile attempt to silence the person—big mistake...*'tis starving makes it fat*. All you will do is infuriate him further. As he's relating the specifics of his injury, repeat back, with empathy, a sentence he just spoke. This shows him that you're listening, and he will feel supported by your empathy. Ask him to repeat part of what he told you, so he or she will vent more. This competency level will put the odds greatly in your favor if you're seeking peoples' cooperation.

A beautifully compelling story comes from Anthony de Mello's book, *The Heart of the Enlightened*. Once upon a time there was an inn called the *Silver Star*. The innkeeper was unable to make ends meet even though he did his very best to draw customers by making the inn comfortable, the service, cordial, and the prices reasonable. So in despair he consulted a sage. After listening to his tale of woe, the sage said,

"It's very simple. You must change the name of your inn."

"Impossible," said the innkeeper, "It has been the *Silver Star* for generations and is well known all over the country."

"No," said the sage firmly. "You must now call it the *Five Bells* and have a row of six bells hanging at the entrance."

"Six bells?" But that's absurd! What good would that do?"

"Give it a try and see," said the sage with a smile. Well, the innkeeper gave it a try. And this is what he saw. Every traveler who passed by the inn walked in to point out the mistake, each one believing that no one else had noticed it. Once inside, they were impressed by the cordiality of the service and stayed on to refresh themselves, thereby providing the innkeeper with the fortune that he had been seeking in vain for so long.

*There are few things the ego delights in more than correcting other peoples' mistakes.*

We are all vulnerable to the allure of the ego, and we all struggle with its spellbinding influences every day. To the extent that we can promote those attributes that appeal to our better selves and let go of our lesser selves will determine how competently and successfully we interact with our fellow citizens. The first step of course, is in making ourselves aware of, and alert to, ego's mechanism and the price we pay in its service. That, I believe, is half the battle.

## The Man in the Ape Suit

It blew my mind! It was the most eye-opening experience I could remember. No, it wasn't an out-of-body spiritual experience; it was a one-minute video-clip. Michael Shermer is the publisher of *Skeptic Magazine,* a magazine that exposes pseudo-science, hoaxes and junk science. He was giving a lecture about perception blindness at the TED (Technology Entertainment Design) Conference where he showed the audience a short video. Before he showed the video he asked the audience to perform a task where he's going to have them do a count as they watch.

There are six students in the video, three with white shirts and three with black shirts. There are two basketballs and they're passing them back-and-forth while they're moving and weaving between each other. The audience's task is to count the number of passes between the white shirted students only, as they move around for one minute. I'll point out here that the area in which the students are moving and passing is no more than ten by ten feet. He tells them that there's an interesting effect where there are gender differences with attention to this kind of detail when there's a lot of action going on.

He tells them he's not going to divulge which gender is more accurate...but we'll see what happens at the end; then he proceeded to show the video. At the end of the showing he asks the audience for some of the numbers they counted and few blurt out their count. Then he asks,

"Anyone see anything unusual, let's have a show of hands; anyone see anything really unusual?"

Well, laughing, about half of the audience raised their hands. I, myself, saw nothing unusual, and all the people I showed the video clip to, also saw nothing unusual.

Then he tells them he's going to show the clip again, but tells them not to count; just watch it globally. I watched again, and unbelievably, a man in an ape suite calmly walks through the scene, right into the middle of the students, stops, and performs a silly gesture as the students are still moving and passing the basketballs.[7] At first, you suspect that the ape-man didn't appear the first time the clip was played, so I had to go back and watch the first clip again. Sure enough, it was the same clip; no switch occurred, the ape-man did enter the scene.

If I were reading about this, as you are now, I would not believe it to be possible. But I'm here to tell you, it is. You most likely can view a similar video by going to Google and enter, *Count the passes on the white team*. By the way, there are no gender differences, Shermer just said that, as he put it,

"To up the ante."

This is called priming the mind where peoples' attention is narrowly focused, or where they acknowledge only certain data to fit their theories. Here was the man in an ape suit walking through the scene, even stopping and making a silly gesture, that I was blind to...how on Earth could I not see what was right in front of my nose?! It was glaring! Professor Richard Wiseman of the University of Hertfordshire recently repeated this experiment before a live audience in London (as part of his Theatre of Science) and found that only ten per cent of the 400 or so people who saw the show managed to spot the ape-man.

This psychological exercise can be used as an outstanding analogy in relation to our egos. Watching only the ball being thrown symbolizes our ego distracting us from perceiving what's right in front of us. The ape-man symbolizes a large part of reality that we cannot see because of the attention the ego is demanding, and blinding us to crucial information.

The ape-man is emblematic of the enormity of information we are distracted from, as the ego promotes a narrowly focused attention onto ourselves—protecting our beliefs, our image, our need to be right, our need to project something we are not, defending our mistakes, self-deception, obstructing a new idea, etc.

As a consequence, our competence suffers terribly from cutting-off data that would otherwise be instrumental in furthering our achievements and personal lives. If you are out to lunch in perceiving what people are trying to communicate to you, or in assessing a particular situation in your life, or business, you are laboring under a severe handicap. The indulged ego is an expensive partner.

The ego has convinced us that who we are is not enough. By buying into this we choose not to allow parts of ourselves to exist and spend large amounts of energy suppressing them.

We all struggle to maintain the integrity of our true selves. We need to get rid of the ego as dictator and transform it into our servant, and in our service. The following section will go a long way in calming down the tyranny of ego, thereby substantially enhancing your effectiveness in the real world. An excellent perspective in utilizing some of these methods is to look at the ego as the activity of your child, which in essence the ego is, an activity. When you recognize its misbehavior, respond by saying to this child,

"Hey, what are you doing? Go sit down, calm down, and behave," as would a parent.

You do not hate that active part of yourself just as you wouldn't hate your child; you're simply molding that child's character because you love him or her. With your guidance, that child becomes more and more competent to function in the real world. By taming the ego, you allow your intellect to guide you in *personal leadership*, rather than handing it off to a spoiled child.

## Taming the Ego: Enhancing Competence

• Extending yourself to people by listening to them, and drawing them out, is an excellent method because the ego is not inquisitive, it doesn't look for new information and is certainly not interested in other people unless there is something in it, for *it*. And, allow yourself to be influenced as we covered earlier, if their thoughts have merit.

• Whenever you find yourself looking down your nose at someone, don't allow yourself to bask in it. You may feel you are more intelligent, more enlightened, more educated, have a better job, have a higher socio-economic status, are more spiritual, morally superior, more important, or any other ego-driven drivel that separates you from others. Cultivate a feeling of connection and of being equal. An Italian proverb says, "When the game is over, the king and the pawn go into the same box."

• Develop a love and passion for truth. What does that mean? It means that you don't cling to a conclusion that's emotionally dear to you, and then go looking for selective facts to support it so your ego feels comfortable and secure. It means to have the courage not to delude yourself, and to seriously entertain new information that doesn't square with your long held treasured beliefs. Socrates said he was happy to be proven wrong because it removed ignorance from his soul. And, one of the best wisdoms about truth I've ever read comes from Friedrich Nietzsche, "Convictions are more dangerous enemies of truth than lies." Revel in new truth.

• Give credit where credit is due. Recognize the talent in people, recognize their greatness and then express it. Rid yourself of the fear that recognizing other people and pointing it out diminishes yourself...it's the ego at work. It is your own greatness that perceives and acknowledges greatness in others. Giving credit comes from strength. Strength equates with self-esteem. Fear along with jealousy equates with ego and weakness.

• *Ego* is Latin for *I*. Notice how many times you use the word "I" in the course of a day. Then try to cut down the number of times you reference yourself and how much time you spend talking about yourself.

• Poke fun at yourself once in awhile. The ego has no sense of humor about itself; it is far too arrogant and pompous.

• Abandon knee-jerk judgment of people. Be cognizant of when judgment kicks-in. Kick it out. Cultivate tolerance.

• Must you win an argument? Why? Occasionally, be kind instead of right. This is one of the most difficult things to do, especially when we're passionate about something. It's easy to have an otherwise constructive conversation deteriorate into a competition, where communication ceases, and a contest begins. When you're upset, people will then mirror your emotional tension triggering a commensurate response and thereby sabotage communication. Try to stay competent, listen and allow the other person's feelings to vent with full expression. Remaining competent through understanding and attempting to make your point again, the competency of everyone concerned is elevated. Religious historian and author, Karen Armstrong, asks, "When you argue, do you get carried away by your own cleverness and deliberately inflict pain on your opponent? Do you get personal? Will the points you make further the cause of understanding or are they exacerbating an already inflammatory situation? Are you really listening to your opponent? What would happen if—while debating a trivial matter that would have no serious consequence—you allowed yourself to lose the argument?"

- Once in awhile, especially if it's not that important, restrain yourself from correcting someone when they make an error. The need of the ego to correct is almost irresistible. When you do resist this urge, you are taking a huge step in taming the ego.

- Take a little time to extend a compliment to another human being. If you look close enough, you'll see a redeeming quality.

- And from the apostle Paul, "Love is patient, love is kind. It does not envy: it does not boast; it is not proud. It does not dishonor others, it is not self-seeking; it keeps no record of wrongs. Love does not delight in evil but rejoices with the truth. It always protects, always trusts, always hopes, always perserveres."[8]

When you start nudging your ego to relax and lighten-up, you start to harmonize your energies with the energies of the people around you, greatly enhancing your *influence over them*, and permitting your intellect to operate optimally for your optimal benefit, and theirs.

*The conversation equated to more of a debate + it was difficult to remove the emotion*

# Non-Adversarial Negotiation: Real or Oxymoron?

*Ever negotiate with lawyers at a huge company? If they saw you drowning 100 feet from the shore, they'd throw you a 51-foot rope and say they went more than half way.*
—Paul Somerson

Any work discussing influencing people would be hard-pressed not to include the topic of negotiation. Being a subject that fills many books, and could fill many more, a comprehensive exploration of the science and art of negotiation is beyond the scope of this book. What we will cover here are some valuable fundamentals that will be quite helpful in the quest of true cooperation. From working in the sales profession, and in my study of negotiation, I've noticed they are closely related; many of the techniques overlap. With that in mind, we need to recognize that there is a fine line between a skillful endeavor toward true cooperation and that of manipulation, therefore, I will try to avoid entering that slippery slope where the former ends and the latter begins.

I believe that the further we get into manipulation, the further we move from true cooperation. It's a tightrope walk, and we must monitor ourselves. As we previously discussed, there are "tells" we all give off in our communication with people, and when we start entering the area of being slick and manipulative, those tells will come through and you become unwillingly and unknowingly transparent. It's much better to come from a position of offering transparency, keeping in mind that people today are savvy and perceptive. We will do well not to underestimate them.

Negotiation, historically, and unfortunately, connotes an adversarial activity; I try to rip something away from you and vice versa. The process has the reputation of being combative, in other words, truly a win/lose, zero-sum situation, and if ego is involved, where only "I" wins, it will remain that way. Because of that distorted view, most people will enter the process with trepidation and anxiety of potential loss, seeing it as a frightening proposition, something not to look forward to and with a tendency to avoid it. Going in with a win/win intention, an attitude of lets solve this together, greatly reduces the stress of negotiation.

Some of the best negotiators on the planet are children. It probably develops within them because the balance of power between them and parents is not in their favor, and it necessitates developing the skill of negotiation as an element in balancing out that power. I remember vividly when I was sitting on the floor having a tough time trying to repair a hole in the wall with a piece of drywall and my daughter Elena coming to me with a request. I believe she wanted to go somewhere with her friends.

The request is somewhat fuzzy in my memory, but the technique she used remains with me like it happened yesterday. I said to her something on the order of,

"Elena, I'm really busy right now, I can't deal with it at this moment, talk to Mom."

She then asked this excellent closing question without batting an eye,

"If it's ok with Mom, is it ok with you?"

*Ultimately we both parties wanted the best the woman*

In my preoccupation with my wall-struggle, I said, "Yes."
Now, what do you think she did? She went and told her mother that,
"Dad said I could go, is it ok with you?"
She closed me with an excellent closing question, and used my agreement as the club to close her mother. Brilliant!

Yes, negotiation can be win/win directed, provided you've developed your listening skills and have done some work to tame your ego. The crucial concept we're after is to set the table in a way that each gets what they want, making it a rewarding experience and infusing the process with power. It seems paradoxical, and therefore difficult for many to get their minds around how this can be accomplished, and that is because of two reasons. One, we think about negotiation as groveling over a *single issue,* as in the price for instance, and two, we enter into negotiation with the mind set that both you and the other person want the same thing.

The latter is an erroneous and dangerous assumption. When two parties prefer different things in the negotiating process, a single-issue confrontation is circumvented. If it gets down to a single issue, it will necessarily transform your dialogue into a win/lose scenario. In other words, if they get what they want, we lose. So, we must avoid narrowing the process into a singular bone-of-contention. We need to realize that we're all unique in our perspectives, we each see a situation from a different angle, what one person wants doesn't mean that's what the other wants as well.

In determining what one wants, we need to start probing for information; what, in fact, do they want,

*mutually agreed solution*

> + her baby to be safe, but we can had a different perspective on the situation

what are some of their problems, why do they want it? Here is where your willingness to listen is paramount, and where, many times you'll be surprised by the answers. Sometimes what they want is much less or different or both, than what we imagined, and therefore easier to agree to. So, in probing and understanding we create options. With more options it is easier for us to come to resolution. Knowledge is power.

Gathering information before mediation begins can aid you enormously in the game of negotiating. Taking someone to a casual lunch is an excellent venue where a person will volunteer a great deal of information and can provide you with a better understanding of what that person wants and needs. Open-ended questions beginning with phrases like, "How did that happen," "Why did you do that," or "How did you feel about that," will give you an intimate sense of this human being. We can learn about the person's family life, hobbies, interests, etc. It exposes what other issues are important to her, including hidden agendas.

Then, when seeking a compromise on a major issue, an ancillary issue can go far in resolving it, avoiding the grinding that a single issue will create.
If you didn't go through this process, you're probably operating out in left field with your assumptions...most likely false assumptions, therefore, it's essential that we know who we're dealing with, specifically what it is that would be important to them, and keeping a few of those issues on the table rather than whittling them down one by one where you've painted each other into a corner of a single issue.

Multiple issues keeps options open, provided both sides have the room to trade-off, leaving each side feeling they both came out winners in the finale. From the point at which you now have accurate information and insight, the process can look to reach a gratifying compromise, insisting on a win/win, with both sides feeling good. Right at this point, I want again to go back to how essential listening is. When we study several negotiation techniques, and then try to utilize them all in the process of negotiating, it will distract us from exercising our listening skills. And that would be harmful to your efforts.

Clouding the mind with too many techniques can be counterproductive. I can understand comprehensively studying techniques when negotiation is a part of your everyday function, however, for our purposes keeping it simple with general guidelines will serve us well. It's important that you are aware of this in the heat of the process; listening will be your most important ally. As an example of getting information in the negotiating process, I was working as a straight commission salesman, and was asked to transfer to another sales territory in Chicago.

The company I worked for wanted me to take over and work this territory, which was wide, and build it far beyond where it ever was. They felt the potential was there. I was quite reluctant, but said I would consider it. I did a little information gathering on the history of the territory and found that it historically had problems of growth, despite the fact that it was large. In fact the area seemed effete. That told me they saw something in my sales ability that could transform the problem territory into a more profitable one.

They had a problem they thought I could solve. Whether the problem was due to the intrinsic value of the territory or that the salespeople working it in the past weren't very competent was an unknown. So with this better perspective of the situation, I wrote up a proposal utilizing a trade-off negotiating strategy. In the proposal, I laid out the rationale that I had worked at my present territory developing it for two years and would be leaving all that leg work and potential business behind, therefore, I would agree to transfer if they would relinquish some of the new territory's existing house accounts as mine to develop further, and those accounts would have an aggregate dollar amount, which I calculated in the proposal.

Further, I would keep my present accounts and any new accounts that came in from my old territory for a period of six months, would be mine, provided I had called on those companies. I sent it to the general manager and he agreed to it and we seemingly both won. In good faith, I pulled out all the stops to develop the new territory and it did in fact provide a higher sales volume than ever before. Both the company and I won. This is a good example of probing for information as to what you're dealing with, and negotiating accordingly, which resulted in a win/win. The process wasn't a white knuckle; drag down fight because both of us saw a benefit. It was a mutually good experience.

Before the negotiating meeting is even scheduled, there is a chance that an impasse could raise its ugly head. They may say, "I want you to know that we have to have such-and-such or we cannot even begin to discuss it." That's where the technique of what I call, "agreement by inertia," is useful. You simply say, "I understand how you feel about that...why don't we just put that aside for the moment and continue with our dialogue."

> Thinking about responding to the conversation can be a distraction. It prevents focus

Now, in the course of the negotiation you can work on solving other minor issues, creating a momentum of agreement toward overcoming the impasse issue—using inertia. As in physics, it's much easier to push a body in motion than it is from a dead stop, and where the dynamic changes because their thinking is becoming more pliable and primed to make some degree of concession on their hard-line position.

The first rules of power in negotiation are a combination of two things. The first of these is the power of your presence. Walk into the room standing tall, give a good firm handshake, make direct eye contact, and as best you can, look relaxed and if possible use some humor. One expert in body language says that he could tell a "wolf" from a "lamb," just by the way they carry themselves, walk and dress. Take a few deep breaths before walking in and just say the word to yourself, "relax."

Second part of the first rule, is being prepared to, and having the willingness to, walk away. You will put yourself in a weakened position if you make up your mind beforehand that you *will* bring this to an outcome. There are few situations where you *must* have it. Entering with the state of mind of being willing to walk away is not negative; it just allows you to operate from a foundation of strength, reducing pressure, giving you a sense of liberation. And it will show in your attitude, your body language, your tone of voice and your tells. You will have a certain sense of assuredness and confidence.

This doesn't mean you go in being cocky. That would be ego-driven and counterproductive. When I use the term "power," it doesn't come from an egocentric place, as in "control over." It means internal power that allows you to function more competently, it means that if you have to, you have the capacity to abort the effort without fear. You do have power.

The second rule is to keep your eye on the ball, focusing only on the issues, not the personalities within the meeting. Stay objective and resist the temptation to become emotionally involved and lose sight of what you're attempting to accomplish. Maintain your perspective.

Some negotiating gurus teach about certain personalities, their traits and how to recognize and deal with them. When I tried to identify my own personality by its parameters and that of my friends, I found that we possess a combination of traits, some of which are identified with *opposite* personalities.
We humans are complex creatures and difficult to delineate so easily. As a result, I find that the task of attempting to identifying personality types is more confusing than it's worth and is a distraction away from listening well, therefore, it's my position that we cut through this cornucopia of data of emotional traits and ideologies in an attempt to decipher them, and focus on what's of mutual interest to the parties involved. The only things that matter in the negotiating process are the issues, nothing else.

In regard to personalities, we need to be cautious they do not dominate the discourse. If that is allowed to unfold, we're operating in dangerous waters. I once worked for a man who was in negotiation for a piece of real estate, a brown stone building that was perfect for his business, the entryway having a beautiful winding staircase that would impress all his clients who would come to visit, and he visualized how it would look with all the arty additions he would put in to enhance its appearance. He and the owner of the property were negotiating on the phone when it precipitated into a heated debate, killing the deal. He has regretted it ever since, often lamenting over the loss.

It was a senseless loss over an ego-personality clash, and he knew he made a mistake, attributing much of the blame to his real estate agent for allowing him to communicate directly with the owner. As we discussed earlier, the danger of having a conversation deteriorate into a contest of winning an argument is the exact same thing that can easily happen in the negotiating process. This is where taming of the ego pays off handsomely. This man's ego got in the way, and his competency suffered. As pointed out earlier, egos are expensive, never paying their way.

At the onset of preparing for a negotiation meeting, we need to address the problem of intimidation you may feel before and during the process. Your posture of having a willingness to walk away will most certainly help you in this regard. When I gave sales presentations to prospects, I always started out with a question. Getting the other person to start talking not only gave me information but it also relaxed me because there's no pressure when you're listening.

As you relax you feel more in control, helping to increase your confidence. Psychologically, business titles exude a certain power that can induce intimidation. Being aware of this reflex response will help you in dismissing that feeling and to begin dissipating it. Titles in the business world are thrown around with ridiculous abandon, and mean nothing in most cases. Realize this person is a fallible human being just like you.

Keeping focused on the issues, instead of on the personalities, carries with it its own power and intimidation. One other thing that's good to know is that your silence creates intimidation. Resist the need to fill every silent gap in the conversation. People are usually uncomfortable with silence and they will nervously try to fill the verbal vacuum; your silence represents control and confidence. I mention this not as a deliberate gambit to be used with everyone, but only when it's necessary, to offset any intimidation directed at you.

As you enter into dialogue it would be constructive to know a psychological principle that says people do things to reinforce a decision they just made. What does that mean to you? It means that the negotiating process will be much easier when you don't ask for everything you want up front. Your odds of agreement are reduced substantially if you ask for everything in the beginning, rather than asking for some of what you want *after* an agreement.

What is happening is that there is a sense of relief that the negotiation process is over, rendering the person vulnerable.

They're relaxed, more flexible, and are now psychologically more confident in their decision than before they made it. Psychological studies have shown *peoples' confidence in their decisions is strengthened merely from the act of making the decision.* That's because they *want* to feel more confident. You can then say something to the effect,

"That does include the such-and-such, right?" You're well aware this is exactly the ploy car salesmen use when they start with the infamous add-ons after the sale is made.

There is a conversational tool that can be used to elicit information that may otherwise be secretive and may come in handy in the course of negotiation. It's called the *sucker punch.* The term comes from the world of boxing where a boxer who has been trained to be an excellent counter-puncher tempts his opponent to throw a particular punch where he's adept at weaving away from, positioning himself and setting his opponent up for the counter-punch. The ploy is to say something that you know is untrue or exaggerated, which provokes the other person to correct you. Remember the story about the *Silver Star Inn,* where the name was changed to *Five Bells—* where the need of the ego to correct is almost irresistible?

This tool exploits that ego need. As a simple example, if you wanted to get a good idea of a private company's annual sales, you might inadvertently mention,

"I heard somewhere your sales are around $10 million,"

knowing that it's probable their sales are far above that. Then just observe what their response is. Chances are good you'll be corrected pronto and may get more of an in-depth explanation than you thought you would. The response would be especially prone to giving up information when your statement triggers a type of defense mechanism.

For instance, let's say an acquaintance of yours had a serious discussion with a group of his friends regarding a disagreement that was threatening the group's friendship, and let's suppose he's being tight lipped about it. You really would like to know what happened, so at an appropriate time you casually mention in a concerned way that you heard he was taken advantage of during the discussion. It will most likely trigger an ego defense mechanism that will open him up and set you straight in how well he handled the situation, therefore, this technique can prove useful when trying to uncover guarded information.

Any points you want to emphasize in the process of negotiation will carry much more weight if you can provide something written to corroborate it with. The reason is psychological, in that there is power in the written word. The point is driven home more powerfully because we tend to believe something more strongly when we see it in black and white, being anything that supports your points, an organizational policy, a magazine article, a book, a newspaper, etc.

Also, there is another important point about the printed word. When an agreement is reached where both sides want to see the agreement in writing, always try to be the one who writes it. The advantage is with the author because many times there will be some minor points that become apparent that weren't covered verbally, and they come to mind when you're crystallizing the agreement onto the written page. The points can then be framed to your advantage, leaving the burden to them if they want to request some minor changes to minor points.

## Utilizing Emotions Toward Agreement

First of all, your own emotions should be welcomed and accepted as valid because they impart information about what's important to you. Suppressing them will make it harder to concentrate on the real issues. We are a society that is taught to hide our emotions, and to be ashamed of them. We can't control our emotions any more than we can control the growth of our hair, so don't feel guilty about having them, nor should they dominate your behavior. Just accept them.

As we've covered in chapter one, emotion is the biasing catalyst that gives us the ability to conclude, to come to decisions. It also sets the tone and the atmosphere when attempting to attain agreement. Psychological research tells us that negative emotions such as anger and fear narrow our attention to a specific action as in fight or flight, whereas positive emotions broaden our thoughts and options.[1] Picture the receptive flexible state of the other person's mind as the aperture of a camera. Infusing him with positive emotions widens the aperture for increased flexibility, and negative emotions squeeze it smaller rendering him rigid.

Just by the definition of negotiation, it's a given we're going in with differences, therefore, why on earth would we exacerbate those differences by not paying attention and inadvertently evoke negative emotions from them? We must interact with them in a way that stimulates positive emotions. Positive emotions allow nonthreatening dialogue about each other's distinct differences. We also discussed the need we all have to feel important, and this feeling of importance is closely associated with the desire to feel appreciated. It feels good to be appreciated, and when we feel good we become more receptive and flexible to those around us.

Simply stated, what we're after is getting the person we're dealing with to be emotionally with us, to whatever degree that is possible in a negotiating scenario, therefore, if we are sensitive and skillful in inducing a feeling of being appreciated into another person, he will be much more receptive and agreeable to us. Just a word or two could make all the difference.

*Validating + understanding the other party's viewpoint is beneficial*

Utilizing this concept in negotiation will foster a win/win scenario with excellent effectiveness. We will again rely heavily on our loyal partner—listening.

When listening to a person's views, instead of automatically seeing them as flawed, we can modify our perspective and recognize the merit of what they are saying. Also, you may discover why the issue is personally important to them, so when they express a point of view that is in contrast to your own, and seemingly an obstacle to agreement, you express understanding. This does not mean you are agreeing with them. Much too often, people are fearful of expressing understanding because they're almost terrified they are conceding.

This is a slight-of-hand we inflict on ourselves that inhibit communication. There is a light-year of difference between not understanding, and *refusing* to understand, one comes from honesty and strength and, the other comes from the fear of giving in. Understanding and agreement are two different things; we need not confuse them. You can understand, and also maintain your position. As in our assurance phrases, understanding validates a person, where you express that you comprehend his point of view, rather than dismissing it.

Now, we will take it a step further. After we express understanding, we then convey its merit. Merit means that you recognize the value in the other person's assessment. The important qualification here is that you actually *do* see merit in his position. Recognizing the merit of his idea is crucial, because we could say we understand, and then patronizingly dismiss it. As an example we could use the issue of making an amendment to the constitution banning flag burning. You disagree with going to that extent. You express to the person proposing it saying,

"It's understandable that you feel offended by this behavior, it disrespects the country we love." *(You understand and appreciate their view)*

"Even with your reverence for freedom of speech, the act of desecrating our flag is a gross abuse of that freedom." *(Your assessment has merit).*

This gives this person immense gratification that his voice is acknowledged and lays the emotional groundwork for coming to agreement. Remember, just as with assurance phrases, it is of paramount importance you remember *never ever* use the word "but" or "however" afterwards.

Building a connection becomes a strong influence in developing a rapport of working together. As we discussed earlier, relating will go a long way in that endeavor. Prior to your building other connections with this person, the only connecting factor you both share is the actual disagreement, so that if things become a little tense, the other connections you have developed act as a cushion. If it's at all possible sit side by side instead of across from each other because it physically symbolizes togetherness toward a common goal. Call attention to the fact that you both share a common task where you might say something to the effect,

"Together, we have a challenge here in solving something both our people will be gratified with." That perspective enables a sense of being on the same team.


Obviously, negotiation is not a love fest. There may be some tense moments in the sincere win/win effort of moving toward agreement. It's a far cry though from the zero-sum game most of us have come to abhor. This kind of negotiating means everyone feels successful and gratified, where there remains a feeling of accomplishment and respect for each other. This is the goal, as in the spirit of cooperation.

# The Power of Cooperation

*The only thing that will
redeem mankind is cooperation.*
—Bertrand Russell

*None of us is as smart as all of us.*
—Ken Blanchard

*Sticks in a bundle are unbreakable*
—Kenyan Proverb

*Thank you for your cooperation.*
—RoboCop


Many times we tend to objectify problems by putting a label on them as if they were things. Some examples would be global warming, drug addiction, pollution and war, and as things, they seem beyond our control. Fundamentally, however, they are not things. In actuality they are actions, or more specifically human behaviors, and it follows that if behaviors give us these problems, then behaviors can eliminate them. In general, new human behaviors can resolve most of our dilemmas, and, cooperation is at the heart of that behavior. As stated in the introduction, when working together, great things happen. Cooperation is power.

I remember watching an episode of *The Untouchables,* the 1959 television series starring Robert Stack portraying Eliot Ness.[1] It was the time of Prohibition, where two Chicago rival gangs owned several speakeasies and breweries. Ness devised a plan to incite a gang war between the two, making his job of wiping them out much easier by causing them to annihilate each other. Setting up a series of raids, he physically tore the businesses apart on only the establishments of one of the gangs. His strategy obviously provoked paranoia into the leader of that gang, leaving him with the notion that the rival gang boss had struck a deal with Ness.

Sure enough, after two or three raids, the stricken gang leader rounded up his mob boys and headed out to the office of the rival leader, bursting into the office with his henchman, seething with rage and ready for war in a New York second he found his rival sitting calmly behind his desk, actually waiting for him with three or four of his knuckle-draggers beside him. Then the rival mob boss spoke. He was smart...he was very smart. He instinctively knew what Ness was up to and calming his thick-skulled Neanderthal competitor down, he began explaining the reality of the situation.

He speaks, "Ya wanna play into Ness's hands Frank? Ya wanna start shooting? These guys beside me could shoot back too, I hired them for 50 bucks each. We could snuff each other out right here. Ness wants us to start a gang war. He would be real happy with that Frank, real happy we were so stupid. Or do you wanna be smart, and we'll beat Ness at his own game?"

"Yeah, whadaya handin' me; how we gonna do that?"

"Whenever Ness raids one of our joints, we build it back together. We work together, even though we're rivals. I help you now to build back the ones he busted up, you help me if he gets to mine, fifty-fifty. There's enough in this town for the both of us to make a fortune. He'll be scratchin' his head wonderin' what the hell's goin' on. That's what we do."

"Uhh, ok."

Here we have the unlikely alliance between two rival mobsters who beat the fuzz with the power of cooperation, at least temporarily.

We can take a lesson from the natural world in the way cooperation can produce astonishing results. It is probably the ideal model of harmony...our bodies, our planet and the universe itself. Our bodies perform trillions of tasks in any given moment, including the production of such a wide array of chemicals; it is a virtual pharmacological factory. A million billion cells undergo thousands of chemical reactions per second, each of them made up of thousands of intricate parts, with innumerable electric impulses darting through the highways of our nervous systems, that work together to function as a whole.

All of these systems operate with absolute precision and exquisite harmony, giving us this wondrous delicate life. Planet Earth encompasses the interplay of gravity, volcanic and tectonic activity that gives forth landmasses, all in a stunning orchestration through millennia to bring forth life. And the universe, so awesome and wondrous, in a perpetual expanding cosmic symbiotic dance that delivered our Earth and flesh and blood, used immense harmonious relationships from such forces as gravity, electromagnetism, and nuclear fission that achieved the astonishing spectacle of existence.

It all offers us a clue as to what great cooperation can mean to humankind. Human cooperation virtually means garnering the efforts of people toward a common purpose and shared gain. Just about everything we own we owe to the cooperative effort of multitudes of people. Our economy, for instance, is not only built on the effort of people, it literally *is* the effort of people. Consider that it takes hundreds, perhaps thousands of people to manufacture and deliver something as simple as a pencil.

From acquiring the graphite from several different countries, to those who manufacture the metal cylinder that hold the eraser, the rubber for the eraser, forming the rubber, harvesting wood, forming the wood, gathering chemicals for the paint, and transporting these components to the end manufacturer, then transporting the product. All these people, in all these industrial organizations and transportation companies, form a network of enormous cooperation.

Science personifies what great cooperation achieves. There is a magnificent synergistic unity of scientific investigation in the quest for truth from all the sciences—astrophysics, quantum physics, biology, geology, and mathematics, just to mention a few. Because of this our scientific knowledge is increasing exponentially, where it's taken ten thousand years to get from the cart to the Wright brothers, and only sixty-six years from the Wright brothers flight to landing on the moon. Through its cooperative alliances and ingenious calculations, science allows us to peer back and examine the infinitely dense sub-atomic particle, much smaller than an electron, that erupted into the cataclysmic explosion called the Big Bang, spewing out its guts faster than the speed of light, spanning thousands of light years in less than a trillionth of a second[2] creating the galactic primordial crucible which makes up *everything* in the universe.

And now, science is on the threshold of solving the Theory of Everything (a quantum theory that encompasses all forces and all matter), as we attempt to reconcile Einstein's Theory of Relativity with Quantum Mechanics along with its eleven dimensions. Relativity explains the world of the very large, and quantum theory the world of the very small, each in complete contradiction to each other, confounding scientists for at least fifty years which now has led us to Superstring Theory and M-Theory (a unified theory that harmoniously unites quantum mechanics and general relativity...previously known laws of the small and the large, that are otherwise incompatible)[3].

As Stephen Hawking related, successfully integrating Relativity with Quantum Physics into a single formula, would be an introduction into the mind of God.

## Science and Religion

Cooperation can come in many forms, only limited by the creativity of the people involved. There is even cooperative thinking now happening between the seemingly irreconcilable chasm of religion and science pertaining to evolution. In his 1996 Pontifical Academy of Sciences Encyclical[4], Pope John Paul II espoused the following,

> [N]ew knowledge has led to the recognition that the theory of evolution is more than a hypothesis. It is indeed remarkable that this theory has been progressively accepted by researchers, following a series of discoveries in various fields of knowledge. The convergence, neither sought or fabricated, of the results of work that was conducted independently is in itself a significant argument in favor of the theory.

In 2009, Pope Benedict XVI in a written message sent to participants of an interdisciplinary congress titled, *From Galileo's Telescope to Evolutionary Cosmology.*

*Science, Philosophy and Theology in Dialogue*[5], stated that cooperation between science and faith benefits humanity. Following are excerpts:

> Questions on the immensity of the universe, its origins and its end, as well as understanding it, do not admit of a scientific answer alone. Those who look at the cosmos, following Galileo's lesson, will not be able to stop at merely what is observed with the telescope; they will be impelled to go beyond it and wonder about the meaning and end to which all creation is ordered. At this stage philosophy and technology have an important role in smoothing out the way towards further knowledge. Philosophy, confronting the phenomena and beauty of creation, seeks with its reasoning to understand the nature and finality of the cosmos.
>
> There is no conflict on the horizon between the various branches of scientific knowledge and of philosophy and theology. On the contrary, only to the extent that they succeed in entering into dialogue and in exchanging their respective competencies will they be able to present truly effective results to people today.

Science is a constant journey of discovery, an evolving proposition in how our physical world works, all through empirical evidence or hypothesis based on preliminary evidence, seeking to expand our knowledge with an eagerness to embrace new insights, to answer old vexing questions. It is fluid, dynamic and relentlessly inquisitive. It does not start with a premise, but follows a path of detection, with the intent of clarifying and unearthing the unknown, influencing even religion, as when Galileo exposed the cosmos via his telescope, and enlightening the disbelieving clergy that peered through it—we weren't the center of the universe.

Religion gives people comfort and hope through their abiding faith and belief and offers an answer to why we are here. Contention seems to arise when religion and science attempt to delve into the other's realm, as when the religious profess scientific claims via selective facts driven by their belief system, and when people of science insensitively try to cross into spiritual philosophy based on their scientific sophistication.

The alternative would be to keep them hermetically sealed from each other just for the sake of avoiding conflict. The price of that would be the absence of any constructive dialogue and interaction that could conceivably lead to new and more harmonious relationships in the quest for understanding. For those theologians who are also scientists, the two are not conflicting or mutually exclusive, they are complimentary, representing the otherwise implausible concept that both can come together and make us all more whole, a perfect example of the third possibility we dealt with in the first chapter.

In reconciling religion's time-line of creation and that of evolution, should it matter *when* their God created the universe? The miracle of creation demands our reverence and awe, and when it began is less important than its great mystery. As to *how* it began, whether it be through instantaneous creation or through a millennia of natural evolvement, does not for a moment diminish the miracle of life. One of the problems is we tend to think of things as absolute, either black or white. In other words, there are only two ways to consider the truth, A or B. If one is considered false, then the other must be true.

To say it another way, denouncing evolution means instantaneous creation is true, and denouncing instantaneous creation means there is no God. What this line of thinking overlooks is the other possibility that both can be true, God *and* evolution and therefore coexist. We can possibly begin the process of uniting science and religion by recognizing that in one profound way, if you believe basically that a *cause* of the universe exists, science supports faith with the fact that the universe had a beginning.

There is so much overwhelming evidence that verifies the event of the Big Bang, that it is now fact; a specific moment that gave birth to the universe having profound and compelling implications; telling us there was creation, the universe was born, and *it*, giving birth to life. That event cries out in no uncertain terms, there was at least one time when the metaphysical interfaced with the physical, from nothing (how does one get their mind around the concept of nothing?) came something. From this point science and religion have common ground, allowing a path to more compatibility, because both the physical and the nonphysical are participants of existence and the miraculous occurrence of inorganic star-stuff metamorphosing itself into organic matter—evolving into conscious human beings—where *we* are literally the universe contemplating itself.

And, in the bizarre indeterminate world of quantum physics, the mere act of observational measurements conducted by scientists of sub-atomic particles, literally changes their behavior, even causing particles to spontaneously materialize into existence; leading some physicists to think this could be evidence of a cosmic consciousness that permeates the universe, exhibiting an inextricable powerful link between consciousness and the quantum world.

Further, with the four fundamental forces of nature, the strong and weak nuclear forces, gravity and electromagnetism being so finely-tuned, just an infinitesimal variance in any of one of them would immediately impact the universe into an environment where life would be impossible. The close tolerances of these forces along with many of the balancing-acts of Earth, such as its perfect distance from the sun and almost perfect circular orbit around it; demonstrates our universe and solar system exists in a "Goldilocks zone," perhaps signifying an intelligence that has customized it for life. Further yet, astronomer Frank Drake in 1961, developed his famous Drake formula to estimate the number of intelligent civilizations that have radio-transmitting technology in the Milky Way galaxy, where using conservative parameters in its formula, calculates there is only a single planet with that capability;[6] making us indeed, quite special.

Yet, on a planet that is 4.6 billion years old, of the hundreds of millions of species that evolved on it for over 3.5 billion years, primitive humans made their debut in the last minuscule fraction of 1 percent of that time. To get a visual perspective of that time line, if the Earth's age was represented by a distance of 1 mile, the amount of time humans have inhabited it would represent about ¼ of an inch. Since that is an astoundingly inefficient and tortured time-line to arrive at man, it begs reason to conclude that the *intent* of a 13 billion year old universe, in an ordinary galaxy among half a trillion galaxies, itself comprised of billions of stars with at least 500 million planets that are candidates for supporting life;[7] was designed and created solely for the purpose of one tiny subgroup of one species on one tiny planet residing at the edge of its galaxy. Rather it strongly intimates a random event than purposeful. As Mark Twain profoundly observed,

> Man has been here 32,000 years. That it took a hundred million years to prepare the world for him is proof that that is what it was done for. I suppose it is. I dunno. If the Eiffel tower were now representing the world's age, the skin of paint on the pinnacle-knob at its summit would represent man's share of that age; and anybody would perceive that that skin was what the tower was built for. I reckon they would. I dunno.

Neither science with all its meticulously calculated observations, knowledge and sophisticated technology, nor religion with its ancient treasured scriptures, deep abiding faith and holy teachers, really knows; but the ever-growing knowledge about our universe continually deepens the mystery and offers a platform with a good degree of overlap between the two in which science and religion can appreciate each others' views more fully; thereby launching them into a more productive dialogue where both can harmonize in examining, revering and understanding, the stunning and majestic, mystery of life.

## Mutualism and Altruism

Cooperative alliance creates a magical element called *synergy*. Synergy says that two can deliver more than the sum of their parts. In other words, two or more working together accomplish much more than them working separately. One of the components of synergy is known as a division of labor, that is, every person doesn't have to do every task, rather, a person can specialize in a particular task, taking advantage of his or her unique abilities and talents *that benefits everyone within the cooperative group,* allowing others to specialize in specific tasks that are congruent with their unique abilities, forming a collective interdependence with superior effectiveness.

The interesting and ironic thing about cooperation is that no matter how beneficial something is to the group, in most cases it won't work unless it benefits the individuals as well. This is known as *mutualism.* So that if doing something is in the group's best interest, it will nevertheless die if it does not benefit the individual as well. In our example of manufacturing a pencil, all these hundreds of people were necessarily benefiting in their cooperation, in order to bring you your pencil, without which, you wouldn't see a pencil.

This is something to keep in the forefront of your mind when seeking the cooperation of a person—he must also be the recipient of a gain. By our very nature, we respond to incentive. I learned this the hard way when I was in the executive search business. As the manager of an office of about twelve people, I was preparing to expand to two offices, where I would oversee both. Among my staff, we had an excellent producer of whom I was counting on to come with me to help build the new office. He was and still is a good friend of mine. We had a close friendship, great rapport and a wonderful mutual respect.

He would be a tremendous asset in starting this new venture, however, when I asked him to come with me to the new office, he declined. Not only was I disappointed, I was somewhat shocked, nevertheless, I respected his decision, didn't press any further, accepted it and left it at that. A few months later we were talking on the phone and the subject came up, and when I asked him why he didn't join me, he uttered these enlightening words,

"Because you didn't offer me anything."

Of course! Why should he risk his current standing and prosperous arrangement for an unknown without incentive? I will never forget those words, because those words opened my eyes and I'm appreciative of his honesty because he taught me a profound lesson.

How naive and dense could I be? Here I am in a thriving business environment teaching sophisticated sales and skilled listening techniques yet I was out to lunch in my request of him. My mistake? I "assumed," because our relationship was so close, he would automatically want to join me just on the strength of our relationship alone. I was under this delusional kumbaya campfire camaraderie that would just magically transport him to my cause.

This story typifies that the cooperative effort must encompass a benefit for individuals, a crucial element for cooperation, and as obvious as it is, as I've learned, it's easy to lose sight of.

Now, this may give the reader a sense of cynicism regarding human behavior, the view that we humans only respond to a *what's in it for me* mentality. This would be a distorted view. We are much too complicated a species for us to arrive at such a speedy conclusion. It implies absolute selfishness, and I don't believe any rational person would conclude that completely selfish people could form the great cooperative systems our societies have built.

The animal kingdom as a whole exhibits an abundance of generous behavior or *altruism*. For example, male chimpanzees as a group will attack predators to protect each other with the risk of great personal injury, and at the risk of being devoured, cleaner fish enter the mouths of much larger fish to remove parasites, a single fish cleaning more than 2,000 mouths a day, vampire bats regurgitate blood to others at risk of dying if three days elapse without consuming blood, ground squirrels sound alarm calls to protect other squirrels alerting predators to their own presence, and Florida scrub jays often stay at home with their parents, sacrificing personal reproduction in order to help raise younger siblings.

Humans likewise shower each other with huge amounts of generosity every day. It's theorized that this cooperative caring behavior was a major player that has moved early man to the dominant species of our planet. Working together, such as hunting large prey as a group provided more food, better protection, better child rearing and improved reproduction.

There is an innate tendency to be fair to each other, even when we first meet, where many times we are eager to help another without any reward to ourselves. Volunteerism is another prime example. We do it because of our inborn compassion and because we feel better about ourselves, promoting self-love (not to be confused with ego), which is a substantial payoff, therefore, when enlisting another's cooperation as an appeal to aid the group as a whole, or to bestow kindness upon a fellow human being, there are times when it can be a powerful motivator for them to comply, in many cases, with enthusiasm. So, cooperation exists within two areas of human behavior, mutualism and altruism, seemingly a paradox. One is motivated by the benefit to each individual and the other through an unselfish giving. Each has its place.

## Genuine Progress Indicator

There is a tool that assesses the social cooperative effort between our economic growth and human well being. They are not necessarily the same. When the Gross Domestic Product (GDP) rises, most of us may think it to mean that our national economic health *and* well being are better. Fundamentally though, it is flawed, and merely a gross tally of products and services sold, both good and bad, and not necessarily a measure of social well-being, because it doesn't differentiate costs from benefits, or productive activities from destructive ones; they're all lumped together.

It fails to measure the physical realities that common sense tells us contribute to enhancing our genuine well being. These contributions are ignored because no money changes hands, and ignores our physical, mental, and spiritual health, the social unity of our households and communities and the integrity of our precious environment. It plays a slight-of-hand masking any breakdown of social structure and natural habitat—actually portraying such breakdown as economic gain. A good analogy of the GDP as the measurement of the health of a nation is like a doctor taking the blood pressure of a patient as the sole indicator of good health.

When the GDP rises, where more money changes hands, it is automatically assumed to be good for everyone. For instance, crime adds billions of dollars to the GDP due to security measures, increased police protection, property damage, and medical costs;

divorce adds billions more through attorney's fees and second households, hurricane Andrew in Southern Florida was recorded as a $15 billion boon, the Exxon Valdez oil spill was still another addition, as is the Iraq war. The GDP counts pollution as a double gain, when it's created and again when it's cleaned up.

From 1973 to 1993 the GDP rose over 50%, but wages declined almost 14%. In the 1980's, the top 5 percent of households increased their real income almost 20%, yet the GDP recorded it as a bounty to all. With this method of measurement, unwanted expenditures caused by accidents, prisons, corporate fraud, crime and toxic waste contamination are undifferentiated from healthcare, sanitation, mass transportation, or housing.

Beneficial functions such as the volunteer and household sectors are ignored, as are ecosystem services like flood control, carbon sequestration, and soil formation.

The GDP is indifferent to, and devalues the human quality-of-life activities such as parenting, elder care, mentoring and volunteerism. For instance, parenting of stay-at-home moms and dads account for nothing in the GDP, yet commercial childcare adds to the GDP.

Enter the Genuine Progress Indicator (GPI), as the above graph illustrates.[8] This is a new measure of economic and social well being of the nation since 1950. It provides a new accounting model that incorporates *sustainable development,* closely measuring those conditions that maintain human well being—the net social profit. The measure helps us answer, *what are the well-being prospects for our children and grandchildren?* First, it broadens the framework to include economic contributions of the family, the community, and the environment. Secondly, it subtracts in monetary terms, any degradation imposed on society, giving us a comprehensive view of the big picture, the whole truth.

A correlation between the GDP as it relates to the GPI would be analogous to the gross profit of a company as it relates to the net profit. For example, if all the financial costs of damage to water, air pollution, and crime were equal to the GDP, no matter what lofty level it reaches, the GPI would be zero—a disaster for our quality of life.

GPI takes into account 26 factors the GDP ignores, and is intended to provide policy-makers, and us, with a comprehensive and accurate barometer on the health of the economy and how our quality of living is changing.

The GPI has been vetted by the scientific community and is used regularly by government and non-government organizations internationally, redefining our progress. As you can see by the graph, our progress has been stagnant. Both of these barometers are comparable because they're both measured in dollars. The GPI is flat, yet the GDP shows us the economy has more than doubled since 1950.

**Genuine Progress Indicator U.S.A.**

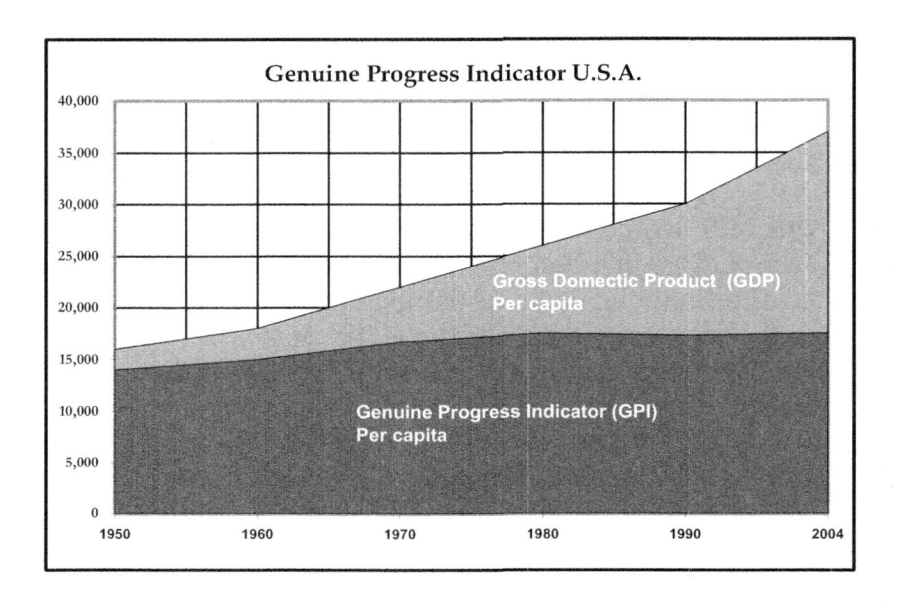

[Chart showing Gross Domestic Product (GDP) Per capita and Genuine Progress Indicator (GPI) Per capita from 1950 to 2004, with values ranging from 0 to 40,000.]

    A salient and disturbing point about the GDP is that it doesn't recognize that nature's services aren't free. For instance, New York had crystal clear fresh water purified for them for decades from the Catskill Mountains, and it was so good they even bottled and sold it. Regrettably, with their continuous population growth, much of the watershed land was being altered and transformed into resorts, farms, and homes; along with all the sewage that went with it, contaminating their wonderfully pure water to such an extent that it couldn't even meet the Environmental Protection Agency standards. New York contemplated building a plant to do the same job their pristine watershed forest was doing.

    The cost would be between six to eight billion dollars, with a $300 million per annum maintenance cost, in contrast to it being free compliments of Mother Nature. The other option was to restore the natural purification capability of the land for $1 billion, which as a bonus, would also facilitate flood control. A no-brainer. Therefore, the GPI gives us a running status of our quality of life as it relates to the economy.

We have achieved more material wealth than at any other time in history, where our personal consumption continues to rise. And yet, the GPI gives us a wake-up call—hourly wages have declined, personal debt has increased, savings rates have declined, and quality time with our families has eroded.

Striking a more cooperative balance between the GDP and societal welfare as reflected in the GPI is of paramount importance for us all. For as much improvement we've experienced in our quality of life through economic growth, there is a threshold beyond which more and more economic growth is counterproductive and our quality of life begins to deteriorate—a reciprocity failure. In 1968 Robert Kennedy said this in his eloquent speech at the University of Kansas,

> We will never find a purpose for our nation nor for our personal satisfaction in the mere search for economic well being, in endlessly amassing terrestrial goods. We cannot measure the national spirit on the basis of the Dow-Jones, nor can we measure the achievements of our country on the basis of the gross domestic product (GDP). Our gross national product counts air pollution and cigarette advertising, and ambulances to clear our highways of carnage. It counts special locks for our doors and the jails for those who break them. It counts napalm and the cost of a nuclear warhead, and armored cars for police who fight riots in our streets. It counts

> Whitman's rifle and Speck's knife, and the television programs that glorify violence in order to sell toys to our children.
> Yet the gross national product does not allow for the health of our children, the quality of their education, or the joy of their play. It does not include the beauty of our poetry or the strength of our marriages; the intelligence of our public debate or the integrity of our public officials. It measures neither our wit nor our courage; neither our wisdom nor our learning; neither our compassion nor our devotion to our country; it measures everything, in short, except that which makes life worthwhile. And it tells us everything about America except why we are proud that we are Americans.

The insanity of the GDP places a zero value on quality of life and the natural habitat. Utilizing the GPI is an excellent scorecard to guide policy-makers, economists, and international agencies to work in cooperative unity with both the economy and human well being. Its measure illuminates the absurd blindness, that the only determinant to measure quality of life is dollars, and elucidates, in fact demands, that the costs of other precious irreplaceable factors must enter into, and balance the equation. The creation of the GPI may be the first step science has taken to address an arena that has long been solely the purview of religion—morality—a morality based on knowledge and defined by human well-being and quality of life, moving mankind toward the elimination of human suffering.

## Tribalism

Humans have lived in small tribes for millennia. Most likely it was critical to the survival of *Homo sapiens*.

The tribe would survive only if each member subordinated his personal desires to the best interests of the clan; depending on each other for mere survival as they shared each other's limited resources, gave spontaneous loyalty to the leader, and exhibited a selfless giving spirit; ensuring the individual a helping-hand in a time of crucial need, as who would come searching for them if they were lost, hurt, or wounded during the hunt. Suspicion of outsiders, and the primitive reptilian drive to acquire more resources, most likely increased their chances for survival in a hostile, unforgiving environment. Tribalism, even in today's modernity, seems to be in our DNA; it's "us," as opposed to "them," and has become problematic as man developed more technologically sophisticated and exponentially more powerful weapons; competing for resources and land on a much larger scale, and reveals itself in nationalism, religious intolerance and racism, where the ultimate ugly excess is war.

People strongly identify with the group to which they belong, and many times are suspect of other groups. Tribalism is insidious; it has so many doors in which to enter that in most cases we're not even aware of participating in it. We see it in a myriad of ways, from different racial groups, income strata, religious belief, national origin, sexual orientation, other country, other village, those that don't look like us, act like us, in violence between gangs, even with organized crime between the "families." Chicago Sun-Times Columnist Neil Steinberg depicts it well when he writes,

> Ten thousand years ago, there was you and your family and the group of people you slept with in a pile for warmth at night. And then there were The Others. The Others were the scary outsiders who

were not you, not your family, not your tribe. They looked different, smelled different, spoke differently and might kill you if they came upon you. Unless you killed them first. This primordial fear underlies all nationalism, all racism, all reluctance to accept those not in your group, on your team, with your company, from your neighborhood.

Like all fears, it has its uses, and humanity took thousands of years to inch away from it. The story of the modern world is the story of overcoming fear of The Other—learning to speak together, to work together, to trade, to interact, despite differences. That's why your clothes come from Guatemala and your neighbor is from Ukraine and we have a black man running for president. But don't be fooled by our modern veneer. Don't be blinded by the glow from all those hand-held electronic devices. Fear of The Other is deep in the bones of many, and it boils up under duress.[9]

Both of my daughters were exchange students, where they lived and went to school in other countries. When we attended the parent orientation meetings, we learned that besides the wonderful growing experience our daughters would gain, along with becoming fluent in a foreign language, the overall mission of the program was attaining the invaluable cultural exchange between peoples. These students would bring back with them a new and more cosmopolitan understanding of the world, and when they become the new leaders, the understanding they acquired would have far reaching benefits in bringing our world closer, away from the "us" vs. "them" tribal mentality and the ignorance that is attendant with it. Better understanding between nations brings with it better dialogue, enhanced communication, and ultimately improved cooperation.

Some years ago, set in a city scene, there was a public service television commercial that depicted a group of teenagers hanging-out with paper bags over their heads. It was obvious, by their behavior, they were all good friends and enjoyed each other; when, suddenly, a burst of wind swishes across them, sweeping the bags from their heads, and for the first time, they experienced the faces of their friends. Half were black, half were white. Ironically, blinded by their newfound vision, they became distrustful and frightened of "the others," who were visually different from them. By the expressions on their faces, they were both confused and stunned; then immediately started to orient and divide themselves into two groups; the color of their skin being the primary determinant of their division with each group glaring at the other with suspicion and fear, their joy and camaraderie lost forever.

This well-done portrayal symbolizes the fear residing within the deeper primitive part of our brains; put there to help ensure our survival as primitive man. That survival mechanism is still alive and well today, mostly unnecessary in modern life; outsiders are enemies, inferior to our tribe, and separatism is the order of the day. Pride, prejudice, and mistrust are the tribe's mantras.

Tribalism incites stereotyping of races, religions, and ethnicity, engendering fear and paranoia of "the others." Identifying with a certain tribe seems to give people a feeling of security, safety, and a strong sense of self. Tribalism though has a dangerous influence, where followers will support a corrupt and inhumane leader if they fear "the other" enough. There are extremes, as in

Africa, where millions were killed in Rwanda, Nigeria, Zimbabwe, Sudan, Congo and Ethiopia.

Tribalism engenders a zero-sum game; *not* I could win and you could win too—unaware of the fact that both can have even more with a cooperating spirit, because when one group subjugates another, the generation of wealth is compromised for both groups; reducing the oppressor's wealth through expenditures in controlling the oppressed, and the oppressed because of the restrictions imposed upon their freedom of action, creativity, and the effort expended in their resistance of being suppressed. Encouraging success for the "other" creates more wealth for both and abates the costly tribal fear.

In an interview on *Meet the Press,* former Secretary of State Colin Powell was interviewed by Tom Brokaw.[10] Powel, with eloquence and passion, presented a profound and poignant story about being a Muslim in America. He told of members of his own party who routinely suspected that any Muslim in America would be affiliated with terrorists. Powell was disturbed by this, and expressed that we cannot go on polarizing ourselves in this manner.

He then relates a story he saw in a magazine about a young Muslim by the name of Kareem Rashad Sultan Khan, an American, who served his country in Iraq, and was killed. The article showed a picture of Kareem's mother at the headstone of her son's grave. The headstone gave his awards—Purple Heart, Bronze Star, and the date of his birth...he was 20, and born in New Jersey. Kareem was assigned to the 1st Battalion, 23rd Infantry Regiment, 3rd Brigade, 2nd Infantry Division (Styker Brigade Combat Team), based in Fort Lewis Washington. At the end of his tour, he was considering re-enlisting or going to medical school. He worked with a medic unit when he first arrived in Iraq. Kareem died in Baqubah, Iraq, of wounds suffered from an improvised explosive device.

Then there is Michael A. Monsoor. Monsoor was a Navy Seal who came from a family of Marines. He died on a rooftop in Ramadi in 2006 with the courage few of us could imagine. He was a Muslim. The citation from his Medal of Honor reads as follows:

> Although only he could have escaped the blast, Petty Officer Monsoor chose instead to protect his teammates. Instantly and without regard for his own safety, he threw himself onto the grenade to absorb the force of the explosion with his body, saving the lives of his two teammates. By his undaunted courage, fighting spirit, and unwavering devotion to duty in the face of certain death, Petty Officer Monsoor gallantly gave his life for his country, thereby reflecting great credit upon himself and upholding the highest traditions of the United States Naval Service.

Gregory Boyd[11] is a pastor, and author of *Myth of a Christian Nation*. In it, he enlightens us with this,

> The kingdom of the world is intrinsically tribal in nature, and is heavily invested in defending, if not advancing, one's own people-group, one's nation, one's ethnicity, one's state, one's religion, one's ideologies, or one's political agendas. That is why it is a kingdom characterized by perpetual conflict.

He adds,

> [N]o Kingdom-of-God citizen should ever place undue trust in any political ideology or program. Nor should they be overly shocked when kingdom-of-

the–world leaders or parties act contrary to Christ's ways.

And further states,

> We *want* to believe that God is on *our* side, supports *our* causes, protects *our* interests, and ensures *our* victories—which, in one form or another, is precisely what most of our nationalistic enemies also believe. So it has been for most people throughout history.

And clarifies,

> Now, I want to be clear: none of this detracts from the important kingdom-of-the-world value of political freedom. Nor is it meant to minimize the tremendous sacrifice many have made, and continue to make, to defend our freedom.

The primordial irrational fear associated with tribalism brings with it a separation mentality, as in, who is more moral, who is the mightiest, who is inferior, who is more patriotic, more enlightened, nobler, who has the better culture; my dogma is superior to your dogma; who has the "true God." All a slight-of-hand that distracts us from the most pressing priorities such as hunger, child slave labor, planetary deterioration, and of course, elusive peace.

In his parable, *The Good Samaritan,* Jesus addresses the tribal mentality of that time. His story was of two bitter enemies, a Jew and a Samaritan; where the Samaritan showed kindness to a fellow human being despite their extreme differences and fear of each other. Jesus deliberately chooses adversaries, teaching that love and kindness are superior to fear. This was really radical thinking for that time; something unheard of, almost beyond comprehension. He gave his listeners a sense of options—your behavior doesn't have to be on autopilot—you can tap into your intellect and compassion to change your world and the world of others, for the better.

A more intense endeavor to move toward cooperation with our fellow countries, world citizens, and fellow countrymen is the key, and the key to cooperation is dialogue. Meaning a *genuine* effort to communicate for the good of all people, with skill; the willingness to compromise, and without an ulterior agenda to aggrandize any one country's or group's position over the other. The first requisite to cooperation, whether with personal interaction or on the world stage, is the *willingness* to pursue it; to know its power. Open communication; listening, questions, more listening, then understanding, leading to more mutual trust, is the work that will pay handsome dividends for us all. Abba Eban said,

When all else fails, men turn to reason.[12]

And cooperation *is* reason.

In honor of the six people who were murdered and fourteen others that were wounded including Congresswoman Gabrielle Giffords in Tucson, Arizona on January 8, 2011, by an unhinged gunman, President Obama spoke at the memorial service for the victims, held at the University of Arizona. In his address, he spoke eloquently about us coming together as a people. The following are some excerpts,

> [A]t a time when our discourse has become so sharply polarized, at a time when we are far too eager to lay the blame for all that ails the world at the feet of those who happen to think differently than we do, it's important for us to pause for a moment and make sure that we're talking with each other in a way that heals, not in a way that wounds.

> We should be willing to challenge old assumptions in order to lessen the prospects of such violence in the future. But what we cannot do is use this tragedy as one more occasion to turn on each other. That we cannot do…that we cannot do.
>
> As we discuss these issues, let each of us do so with a good dose of humility. Rather than pointing fingers or assigning blame, let's use this occasion to expand our moral imaginations, to listen to each other more carefully, to sharpen our instincts for empathy and remind ourselves of all the ways that our hopes and dreams *are bound together.* (italics mine)
>
> We recognize our own mortality, and we are reminded that in the fleeting time we have on this Earth, what matters is not wealth, or status, or power, or fame, but rather, how well we have loved, and what small part we have played in making the lives of other people better.

Arriving at agreement with each other carries the greatest hope for happier and more successful lives. Pursuing cooperation recognizes the humanity in all of us because we're more alike than we are different. Fueled by the ego, our tribalism mentality offers us only division, where we lose sight of the incontrovertible fact that we all came from the same place and all made from the same star-stuff.

Entering outer space and looking back at the tiny blue speck that is Earth awakens us with a visual enlightened sense that there is no "them," it's just "us," especially if we were to encounter intelligent life elsewhere in the universe. That would really bring it home. Then, the tribe would be planet Earth, "us", and the extraterrestrials would be "them."

Whether we're child or adult, man or woman, black, white or brown, gay or straight, American, European, Asian, African, whatever religious beliefs or none, we all want the same human gratifications life has to offer—they're no secret—respect, dignity, kindness, to feel appreciated, sharing, the opportunity to pursue our dreams, become educated, and the opportunity for personal development. We can all help each other through a cooperative effort with a greater sense of togetherness, and compassion. The effort to reward ratio is off the chart to the upside; to *our* great benefit.

## Our Environment

On a grander scale we can look at man's relationship and cooperation with his physical world; the world which sustains him with such immense diversity and abundance. We now have awakened to the fact that as large as our planet is, its resources are limited. To illustrate the fragility of our planet's systems, consider the following; the earth is about 8,000 miles in diameter, and the depth of breathable atmosphere is no more than 5 miles. To give a perspective of just how thin that is, imagine a ball four feet in diameter wrapped in a large single sheet of regular copy paper, the thickness of that paper represents the depth of breathable atmosphere in relation to the ball.

Cooperation with our ecological systems, and conserving them, work to our great advantage and benefit, and has become glaringly apparent that in order for our planet to continue sustaining us with any degree of quality, we need to sustain *it* as well. We must keep the golden-goose healthy. So far, our cooperativeness with our planet has been somewhat, shall we say, one-sided, and we may be suffering under the delusion that nature revolves around us, rather than we around *it*. We have been feeding off it while trashing it; for instance we use our oceans both as a pantry and a toilet—not an especially cooperative relationship.

Common horse sense tells us that a one sided relationship is doomed to be temporary. Sooner or later, probably sooner, as in any personal, business, or family relationship, the giver will no longer comply with the taker. In a personal relationship, we can recognize certain signals that warn us something is amiss, provided our ego is tamed enough to allow perceiving it, or even wants to. There may be signs of an emotional distance, or a mood of alienation. As a result of disrespecting and abusing the very bosom that nurtures us, Mother Earth likewise is exhibiting clear signs of alienation. When we practice this with personal or business relationships and lose them, we can move on to other similar relationships; in the case of our precious environment, we cannot stop the world and get off; it's the only one we have.

Indeed, there are many clear signs of alienation as we're impacted with glaring consequential changes that warming is manifesting on our planet. Looking at just a few, we see that NASA scientists estimate that Greenland is losing 100 billion tons of ice each year, and satellite analysis shows that its melt area has increased by 30 percent. In August of 2010, a massive chunk of ice four times larger than the island of Manhattan broke away from Greenland's Petermann Glacier. Climate scientist and glaciologist, Dr. Konrad Steffen, with the University of Colorado has been conducting research in Greenland for the past twenty-five years, and estimates that if Greenland's melting continues at its present rate, sea levels could rise three feet by the year 2100, flooding parts of cities like New York, Miami and Shanghai, and displacing millions of people.

Another sign is the wildfires in the western United States that have increased by 78 days or 64 percent in the past thirty-years. Western fires have become monstrous, and recorded history shows nothing of the magnitude we're seeing today. Since 1999, ten of the busiest fire seasons occurred. A 100,000-acre fire was considered huge ten to fifteen years ago, where one or two a year was unusual. Today a 200,000-acre fire is common. In fact they're even seeing 500,000 and 600,000-acre fires. And while California burns, Florida is sinking 1½ inches every year.

Then, there is Lake Chad, surrounded by Nigeria, Niger Cameroon, and Chad, once the sixth largest lake in the world (25,000 square kilometers). This lake has shrunk 90% in thirty-years, and the thirty million people who live in the area are now forced to compete for its water and fish.

The seriousness of climate change also has the Pentagon highly concerned. In 2003, the legendary defense advisor, Andrew Marshall, head of the Pentagon's secretive think-tank, *Office of Net Assessment*, commissioned a study examining the national security impact of global warming. The report, titled *An Abrupt Climate Change Scenario and its Implications for United States National Security,* informed the Department of Defense that climate change could increase geopolitical conflicts, even wars, over natural resources such as water, food, oil, and natural gas. The report conservatively states that its findings "although not the most likely, is plausible," and that,

> Ocean, land, and atmosphere scientists at some of the world's most prestigious organizations have uncovered new evidence over the past decade suggesting that the plausibility of severe and rapid climate change is higher than most of the scientific community and perhaps all of the political community is prepared for.

It also states, that despite the view of optimists who feel we have the time to outpace climate change with technology,

> This view of climate change may be a dangerous act of self-deception, as increasingly we are facing weather related disasters—more hurricanes, monsoons, floods, and dry-spells—in regions around the world.

The key findings of the Fourth National Climate Assessment for U.S., NCA4, Vol. II (2018), a team of 13 federal agencies, was put together with the help of 1,000 people, including 300 leading scientists, roughly half from outside the government states:

- Human health and safety, our quality of life, and the rate of economic growth in communities across the U.S. are increasingly vulnerable to the impacts of climate change.

- The cascading impacts of climate change threaten the natural, built and social systems we rely on, both within and beyond the nation's borders.

- Societal efforts to respond to climate change have expanded in the last five years, but not at the scale needed to avoid substantial damages to the economy, environment, and human health over the coming decades.

- Without substantial and sustained global efforts to reduce greenhouse gas emissions and regional initiatives to prepare for anticipated changes, climate change is expected to cause growing losses to American infrastructure and property and impede the rate of economic growth over this century.

The Earth, with its energy, water, land, and biodiversity, can provide us all with what we need long-term, provided we have the wisdom to recognize and do what's necessary to guarantee sustainability. There is no imperative that is written in granite preventing us from our own demise, yet our present trajectory, further accelerated with China, Indonesia, and India's "help", may well spell global collapse. The choice of global cooperation is ours to make. We need to listen to what nature is telling us, and question ourselves.

Jay Leno, on his *Tonight Show,* had a segment called, *What Did You THINK Was Gonna Happen?* In one of these segments, he showed a video of a young man straddling directly over a lit bottle rocket with one foot on the front bumper of one car, and the other on the back bumper of a second car. The rocket then fires off with rapid force and hits him squarely in the groin, and sticks, and he falls backward to the ground screaming with flames shooting out of his crotch; then Jay comes on and says,

"What did you think was gonna happen?" as the audience roars at the brainless act.

Applying this as an analogy to our planet; consider that carbon dioxide is an important and harmless gas that we exhale, and plants use in the process of photosynthesis to produce oxygen, and, as a scientific fact, it also has a unique property, it's extremely efficient at trapping and retaining the Sun's heat more so than most other gases—being a greenhouse gas—therefore, the greater percentage of it in the atmosphere, the warmer the air becomes.

And, we can take a powerful lesson from our planetary neighbors, Mercury and Venus in this regard—the average distance of Mercury from the Sun is 36 million miles, and its average temperature is 355 degrees Fahrenheit. The average distance of Venus from the Sun is 67 million miles, and its average temperature is 900 degrees Fahrenheit. So we have Venus at almost twice the distance from the Sun as Mercury, and its temperature is almost three times as hot, seemingly contradictory to common sense...how could that be possible? It turns out that Venus's atmosphere is 96% carbon dioxide ($CO_2$), super efficient at those levels in capturing and preserving the Sun's heat creating a greenhouse effect on steroids; and, back here on Earth, we are spewing this gas into our atmosphere at the astounding rate of 40 billion metric tons per year decade after decade; and as a result $CO_2$ concentration in our atmosphere has risen from 280 ppm in the preindustrial age to 410 ppm at present, a 47 percent increase. So, using Jay Leno's line, *"What Do We THINK Is Gonna Happen?"*

There are many egos in the world that insist on remaining in denial mode, shutting out all incoming information to protect their own beliefs, agendas, and ideologies. They are like the man who falls off a cliff, and as he plummets, he's heard to mutter, "So far so good."

Imagine if science and religion were to come together in collaboration and cooperation, united in the quest of the stewardship of our environment, one contributing inspiration, and the other, knowledge. When it comes to our precious world, we must get beyond the narrow thinking that religion is only about the spiritual, and science is only about the physical, because our environment is both spiritual *and* physical. Merging both could perhaps give us a decent chance toward resolving the problem, and may even be powerful enough to produce a small miracle—get Congress to move boldly—and provide environmental leadership to the world by our example.

Cooperating and respecting Mother Earth's delicate systems will be an investment of incalculable benefit to each of us, especially our progeny, and will make the Louisiana Purchase Treaty[13] seem like we got fleeced.

## Belief Systems

John F. Kennedy said,

"The great enemy of truth is often not the lie—deliberate, contrived, and dishonest—but the myth—persistent, persuasive, and unrealistic." And, it is worth repeating Friedrich Nietzsche's words,

> Convictions are more dangerous enemies of truth than lies.

These convictions come from belief systems; something we all have in one form or another. A belief system can be thought of as the mental acceptance of a proposition, statement, or concept as true on the grounds of apparent authority, which does not have to be based on actual fact. Many of these beliefs, ideas, or convictions have been programmed into us since childhood, many of them without any basis of reason, where hope and wishful thinking are mistaken for knowledge; and become powerful because they are a large part of our identity, and thus have great influence over our lives.

Belief systems are usually rigid rather than flexible, narrow rather than broad, closed rather than open, and immobilizing rather than liberating. When left unchecked, our strongest belief systems can blind us to reality, and become one of the great impediments to cooperation and problem solving.

It is our belief systems that we use to make judgments about the world and about any given situation as being true, good, bad, happy; where we become so emotionally invested in protecting them, facts to the contrary are rendered invisible; seeing only what aligns with and supports our beliefs. They tend to make us think in binary terms, either right or wrong, good or bad, moral or immoral, whereby knee-jerk conclusions are drawn; painting things with a broad brush into gross generalizations in a frail and lazy misguided attempt to simplify the complexities and nuances of life.

The conscious mind may want to make logically precise decisions, yet the unconscious mind wants to feel good. There are times when we know down deep that we are in conflict with our own intellect and common sense when defending our beloved belief system. We turn our back on, and abandon our intellect in order to cling to, and protect, our precious ideological comfort zone, disallowing ourselves to know what we know. If we resist and dismiss that "annoying" nudge, and doggedly continue along the same path of thought out of shear pride and allegiance, we dishonor and deny our intellect, our inner voice, and the integrity of our true and better selves. Neuroscientist and brain researcher, Paul MacLean laments,

> You know what bugs me most about the brain? It's that the limbic system, this primitive brain that can neither read nor write, provides us with the feeling of what is real, true, and important.

The operative word in Dr. MacLean's quote is *feeling,* infused with certainty based on our belief, then becoming our option to either engage our intellect as to the veracity of that feeling, or just blindly and passively ride with it. Intransigent belief constructs a mental barrier to further knowledge and understanding; where nothing, not even irrefutable evidence, will cause it to consider or yield to that information. A great example of this in action happened when I was watching the Rachel Maddow Show airing from Alaska in 2010 when Joe Miller was running for Senator. She interviewed some of his supporters on the street protesting against Eric Holder the Attorney General, regarding and opposing his position on gun control, as they perceived it. She asked one woman holding up a Joe Miller campaign sign,

"Can I just ask, why are you upset about Eric Holder?"

She replies, "I know that he is anti-gun."

Rachel, "What has he done that's anti-gun?"

The woman then utters these vacuous words, "I *don't have all the facts* but I *know* that he is anti-gun."

Rachel asked a man participating in the rally the same question; he replied,
"I don't know enough about that to answer that truthfully, Rachel."[14]

These people who behave solely from the feeling they receive from their limbic system that Paul MacLean depicts in the above quote, do so without the slightest inclination of pausing or questioning it with their intellect, and gather information. This immediate functionality of the limbic system served our primitive ancestors well ensuring their survival by allowing them to react swiftly in the face of imminent death, bypassing the slower conscious assessment of a perilous situation, providing an instantaneous interpretation to environmental stimuli—no conscious thought necessary. This primitive responsiveness lives within us still, and doesn't serve us well interpreting modern world problems unless we make the effort to consciously assess those feelings bubbling-up from our primitive brain.

Bertrand Russell, one of the twentieth century's most influential intellects, insightfully recognized the unchallenged power of the limbic system when he wrote,

> [I]t is curious how people dislike the abandonment of brutish impulse for reason.

And, Mark Twain observes,

> The trouble with the world is not that people know too little, but that they know so many things that ain't so.

It takes courage to be uncertain because doubt leaves the door open, and openness to investigation leaves us vulnerable to the unknown, where the renunciation of absolute certainty is the most difficult step toward intellectual freedom. The 18th century French philosopher Voltaire said,

> Doubt is not a pleasant condition, but *certainty* is an absurd one.

As enlightening and insidious as Dr. MacLean's insight is, we nevertheless have the ability to identify our own illogical fallacies, and can therefore, if we choose, manage them with deliberation—we can disown flawed beliefs and replace them. And yes, it requires considerable fortitude to challenge long held beliefs; they are comfortable, perhaps loyal to a particular group, familiar, and cherished, and can even conjure up warm memories of the way it was, carrying the baton for the people we love or loved. Beliefs can also come from self-serving bias, self-deception, and fuzzy thinking; in short, an integral part of the culture in which we were raised and conditioned. When we dare to challenge them we feel the fear of the unknown as we venture beyond what we previously established as our safe boundaries. We must take heart, however, and remember that the realm of the unknown is precisely the place where solutions to unsolved problems are found.

As Ayn Rand points out in her book, *Philosophy: Who Needs It,* we all need a philosophy,

> Your choice is whether you define your philosophy by a conscious, rational, disciplined process of thought—or let your subconscious accumulate a junk heap of unwarranted conclusions [and] false generalizations...

There are huge dividends in examining our beliefs and putting forth deliberate effort of sound, reflective thought—it brings us closer to the truth—though it can be frightening. This does not mean we abandon our intuition…our inner voice; it does mean we use it along with *good information,* and in doing so; we open up the potential to become both more competent and more liberated. Acting on knowledge works far better than acting on belief. Alexander Green writes,

> Genuine faith is belief in the absence of evidence, not belief in spite of the evidence.

Take health as an example. If a person has a belief that says genetics is the only factor that dictates health, and never examines if that is really true, he or she will most likely miss the opportunity to enhance his or her health and have a more enjoyable life. If they allowed themselves to look at some hard information about vibrant health, they will discover that behavior is the primary determinant to their physical status, not genetics,[15] they then are much more likely to take control and create a much healthier, joyful life. Leader of the Human Genome Project, Eric Lander, denounces genetic determinism with the following quote,

> People will think that because genes play a role in something, they determine everything. We see, again and again, people saying, "It's all genetic. I can't do anything about it." That's nonsense. To say that something has a genetic component does not mean it's unchangeable.

Another example belief is one that is told to children; that if they don't receive good grades they won't be successful in life. If that child, after internalizing this limiting belief, in fact *does* finish school with poor grades, he or she is much more likely to accept that success is something they cannot achieve...a self-fulfilling prophecy; when in fact, many eminently successful people didn't get good grades in school, and many multi-millionaires never finished school. Some notables are Walt Disney, Bill Gates, Mary Kay Ash, Mark Zuckerberg, Woody Allen, Steve Jobs, Michael Dell, George Eastman, Benjamin Franklin, Quentin Tarantino, Richard Pryor, Peter Jennings, Henry Ford, Richard Branson, and John Rockefeller Sr. Then there is geneticist and entrepreneur, John Craig Venter, who has developed the first artificial self-replicating cell in the lab—artificial life, and one of the first who mapped the human genome; carried Cs and Ds on his eighth-grade report cards, and says he was a horrible student in high school, not good at any subject material. It wasn't until he became a medic in the Navy serving in Vietnam that he was inspired to return to school and pursue a career in medical research. He was named in *Time* magazine's list of the 100 most influential people in the world in 2007 and 2008. Human beings are far more dynamic, profound, and complex to have their potential, worth, and spirit measured solely on the basis of school grades.

In his book, *What Intelligence Tests Miss,* Keith Stanovich describes the mental temperament that leads to highly effective cognitive effectiveness,

> The tendency to collect information before making up one's mind, the tendency to seek various points of view before coming to a conclusion, the disposition to think extensively about a problem before responding, the tendency to calibrate the degree of strength of one's opinions to the degree of evidence available, the tendency to explicitly weight pluses and minuses of a situation before making a decision,

and the tendency to seek nuance and avoid absolutism.

Removing and replacing these restrictive, even enslaving beliefs with good information would have a massive positive impact on many peoples' lives. Hard and fast belief systems tend to make us react automatically to certain new information...sort of a robotic reflex-action, similar to the fight-or-flight syndrome, circumventing our invaluable intellect to analyze objectively; where new information bypasses the intellect, surrendering it over to the primitive brain, similar to a short circuit in an electrical system which bypasses the functional circuitry. That mechanism, left unchecked, locks us into a mental state, surreptitiously slipping by our awareness that we *do* have a choice. And choice is our greatest power.

Developing the fortitude to hold those beliefs up to scrutiny removes the sentry at the gate of our minds whose role it is to filter out all information that doesn't align with, protect, and caress our old beliefs. I remember watching supermodel and actress Lauren Hutton in an interview on the *Johnny Carson Show*, when she stated that she's attracted to men who exhibit *mental bravery,* that is, men who are unafraid to admit when they're wrong, or will intrepidly hold their beliefs up to scrutiny and reassess their position when they are presented with compelling information. Their intellectual honesty was appealing to her because she perceived them as secure and strong enough as men to face down their male egos and welcome thoughts differing from their own that exhibit merit.

Belief systems edit our reality and can be a barrier to discovery, especially when they mutate into an ideology or dogma, causing us to distrust any idea that is outside of its doctrine; limiting us from learning. In conceding to dogma, we close off our most precious gift—our minds—to new evidence, forfeiting our choice to be a free thinker. Dogma being the petri-dish which cultivates unthinking, where your views are arrived at by default, denying yourself the liberty of forming and asking critical questions endeavoring to mine for truth; to unveil an untruth.

We wholly empower ourselves by becoming free thinkers. It's of paramount importance that we are prepared to detach from our belief systems when we recognize good information screams foul, because they govern our behavior and determine our decisions through life; being on constant vigil for what we *want* to believe is true, isn't the driving force for *what* we believe is true; and entails pausing, and consulting our intellect, always. The bottom line is developing the courage to be *intellectually honest with ourselves*.

Life is such an enigma with all its paradoxes, ironies, and convoluted twists, when at times even common sense becomes counterintuitive to truth. With infinitely more unknowns than knowns, none of us is privy to what life really is, and because of that, none of us comes remotely close to possessing ultimate wisdom to always know the truth, therefore, it is imperative that we each continually reevaluate our belief systems in order to protect our thinking from becoming ossified; keeping in mind that veracity not only involves accepting as true or not accepting as true, but also in suspending judgment.

What you believe, and why you should believe it, is in actuality a scientific question; believe because it is supported by evidence and verified by experiment, believe it because years of substantiation has given it credence...believe it because your *intellect* tells you it's true, while being prepared to modify your position if new evidence arises.

With all the contentious issues before us such as health care reform, global warming, and abortion, a safe bet we can all count on is that the truth lies somewhere between the two conflicting views. And perhaps "believe" is an inappropriate word to use, rather "just follow the evidence" serves us far better.

Bertrand Russell enlightens us with these profound and provocative words about the courage of honest thought,

> Men fear thought as they fear nothing else on Earth—more than ruin, more even than death. Thought is subversive and revolutionary, destructive and terrible, thought is merciless to privilege, established institutions, and comfortable habits; thought is anarchic and lawless, indifferent to authority, careless of the well-tried wisdom of the ages. Thought looks into the pit of hell and is not afraid...Thought is great and swift and free, the light of the world, and the chief glory of man. But if thought is to become the possession of many, not the privilege of the few, we must have done with fear. It is fear that holds men back—fear lest their cherished beliefs should prove delusions, fear lest the institutions by which they live should prove harmful, fear lest they themselves should prove less worthy of respect than they have supposed themselves to be. [16]

We come much closer to great cooperation when we question our treasured beliefs, learn to honor and revel in truth, and rely on the gift of our intellect and the courage to use it in leading us there, "The greatest obstacle to discovery," says historian Daniel Boorstin, "is not ignorance—*it is the illusion of knowledge.*"

## In Conclusion

Engaging in the skill of influencing people to create cooperation can be life-altering. A new understanding of another person, or the feeling that someone important in your life has a new understanding of you can be intoxicating. It enhances all areas of life. Using cooperative strategies with children and teenagers can make a dramatic difference in their self-esteem; alleviate some of their emotional confusion, and perhaps even head-off a disastrous crisis. Within marriage and romantic relationships, it will deliver a much greater feeling of oneness, connectedness, and emotional security as it relates to that relationship.

With political leadership relations it could mean the difference between going into battle or entering into a new mutual benefit. In business of course, a fatter bottom line. Even in our sexual lives, intimate communication about sex most likely will result in a new cooperation that can lead to heightened sexual levels. In fact, that kind of dialogue, in and of itself, is one of the most intensive foreplay sessions one can have. Cooperation says,

"If we keep doing what we've always done, we're going to get what we've always gotten. Let's replace our battle hats for progress hats, despite the fact that our philosophical views differ. Let's get out of debate mode; let's abandon the contest and the need to win, and deliver some results...we can resume our age-old ideological argument later. When the spirit of all concerned is on-board toward solution, the problem is already half solved."

As mentioned earlier, the first giant step is to create a willingness to pursue cooperation toward a common good. We can appreciate each other's views and recognize value in them, and at the same time disagree. Cooperation makes our lives a great deal easier and much more enjoyable; though not a panacea, it comes close, therefore, making the effort to acquire a few skills in developing it, seems a lot more desirable than seeking dominance over others with all the conflict that is attendant with it.

Cooperation is power, and much superior to force. As in physics, force creates counter-force and therefore has its limitations. Force moves against something, power does not. Power doesn't need to demand. Cooperation unifies, force polarizes and is a win/lose scenario rather than win/win. Loss through force creates foes that lie in wait to even the score, therefore force is constantly in defense mode, whereas cooperation creates harmony. Such is the power of cooperation.

Whatever challenges we face, we can meet them much more confidently at the level of cooperation. As we evolve, cooperation's unifying nature has the potential to transform our world into a utopian place.

# Bibliography

## Feelings and Logic

[1] Charles Darwin, *The Expression of Emotion in Man and Animals,*

[2] *The University of Chicago Chronicle,* February 20, 1997, Volume 16. No. 11

[3] *Teen Times,* Nov/Dec, 1979  Ray Houghton, M.D.

[4] Antonio Damasio, *Descartes' Error: Emotion, Reason, and the Human Brain.*
Damasio is David Dornsife Professor of Neuroscience at the University of Southern California. His research has helped to reveal the neural basis for the emotions, and has shown that emotions play a central role in decision-making.

[5] *Washington Post Foreign Service,* February 10, 1999, p. A19

## Strategies of Emotional Connection

[1] Rosenthal, R., & Jacobson, L. 1968. *Pygmalion in the classroom.* New York: Holt, Rinehart & Wnston

[2] Langer, E., Blank, A. & Chanowitz, B. (1978). The mindlessness of
ostensibly thoughtful action:  the role of placebic information in
interpersonal interaction.  Journal of Personality and Social Psychology,
36, 635-642.

[3] Thomas L. Friedman. World-renowned author and journalist, *New York Times* financial reporter specializing in OPEC- and oil-related news. Previously, he served as chief economic correspondent in the Washington bureau and before that was the chief White House correspondent. A three-time Pulitzer Prize winner, he has traveled hundreds of thousands of miles reporting the Middle East conflict, the end of the cold war, international economics, and the worldwide impact of the terrorist threat. His foreign affairs column, which appears twice a week in the *Times*, is syndicated to seven hundred other newspapers worldwide.

[4] Bettinghaus and Cody (1994) and Foot (1997)

[5] Amygdala Response to Happy Faces as a Function of Extraversion, *Science, June 21, 2002*

[6] Toepfer, S. and Walker, K. (2009). Letters of Gratitude: Improving Well-Being through Expressive Writing. *Journal of Writing Research, 1*(3), 181-198.

## Ego and Competence

[1] Article, *Executive Coaching Secrets for Taming Your Ego – The High Cost of Ego,* Maynard Brusman

[2] Fortune 143.9, April 30, 2001, p.76, *Get Over Yourself: Your ego is out of control,* by Patricia Sellers.

[3] Book, Ayn Rand, *The Virtue of Selfishness*

[4] Book, Deepak Chopra, *The Path to Love: Spiritual Strategies for Healing.*

[5] Book, Dr. Connell Cowan and Dr. Melvyn Kinder, *Smart Women Foolish Choices,* p154

[6] *The Power of Intention,* Dr. Wayne Dyer, PBS Special, March, 2004.

[7] Research conducted by Dr. Daniel Simons of the University of Illinois and Dr. Daniel Levin of Vanderbilt University.

[8] 1 Corinthians 13:4-7

## Non-Adversarial Negotiation: Real or Oxymoron?

[1] Research by Barbara Fredrickson, *The Role of Positive Emotions in Positive Psychology: The Broaden-and-Build Theory of Positive Emotions. American Psychologist,* 56,218-26, 2001.

## The Power of Cooperation

[1] Eliot Ness (1903 – 1957) Prohibition agent. Ness is famous for his efforts to enforce Prohibition in Chicago. He created and led the legendary team nicknamed *The Untouchables.*

[2] Book, *The Grand Design,* Stephen Hawking, Leonard Mlodinow. Page 129.

[3] *The Elegant Universe,* by Brian Greene, string theorist. Pages 422 and 423.

[4] Address of Pope John Paul II to the Pontifical Academy of Sciences

(October 22, 1996), *Truth Cannot Contradict Truth.*

[5] Message of His Holiness Benedict XVI to Archbishop Rino Fisichella, Rector Magnificent of the Pontifical Lateran University, *"From Galileo's Telescope to Evolutionary Cosmology. Science, Philosophy and Theology in Dialogue"* [30 November – 2 December 2009]

[6] Book, *The Singularity is Near*, Ray Kurtzweil p.347
Drake formula: Number of radio-transmitting civilizations =
$$N \times f_p \times n_e \times f_l \times f_i \times f_c \times f_L$$

$N$ = the number of stars in the Milky Way galaxy

$f_p$ = the fraction of stars having orbiting planets

$n_e$ = average number of planets orbiting those stars

$f_l$ = planets capable of sustaining life, number where life evolves

$f_i$ = for planets that sustain life, number where intelligent life evolves

$f_c$ = for planets with intelligent life, number that transmit radio waves

$f_L$ = the fraction of the universe's life which an average communicating civilization communicates with radio waves

[7]*Cosmic Census Finds Crowd of Planets in Our Galaxy,* Associated Press, February 19, 2011. Kepler space telescope, Kepler Principle Investigator, NASA Ames Research Center, William Borucki

[8] Statistics from *The Genuine Progress Indicator 2006: A Tool for Sustainable Development,* at Redefining Progress, Oakland, CA, Sustainability Indicators Program. Authors, Dr. John Talberth, Director of Sustainability Indicators; Cliff Cobb senior fellow at Redefining Progress; and Noah Slattery research fellow at Redefining Progress.

[9] Article, *Stoking Fear of The Other,* October 12, 2008, Neil Steinberg, *Chicago Sun Times.* Mr. Steinberg has also written for a wide variety of publications including *Sports Illustrated, The New York Times,* and *Rolling Stones.* He has also written for many web sites such as Salon and Forbes.com, and is the author of six books. His most recent book is a memoir of his struggle with alcoholism titled, *Drunkard.*

[10] *Meet the Press,* October 19, 2008

[11] Book, *The Myth of a Christian Nation.* Gregory Boyd is the founder and senior pastor of *Woodland Hills Church* in St. Paul, MN, and founder and president of *Christus Victor Ministries.* He was a professor of theology at *Bethel College* (St. Paul, MN) for sixteen years. Pastor Greg Boyd is a national and international speaker at churches, colleges, conferences, and retreats, and has appeared on numerous radio and television shows. He has also authored and coauthored fourteen books prior to *The Myth of a Christian Nation,* including *Escaping the Matrix (with Al Larson), Seeing Is Believing, Repenting of Religion,* and his international bestseller *Letters From a Skeptic.*

[12] Abba Eban (1915-2002). 1966 to 1974 was Israel's Minister of Foreign Affairs. Renowned orator, and fluent in ten languages

[13] Robert Livingston and James Monroe closed on the sweetest real estate deal of the millennium when they signed the Louisiana Purchase Treaty in Paris on April 30, 1803. They were authorized to pay France up to $10 million for the port of New Orleans and the Floridas. When offered the entire territory of Louisiana—an area larger than Great Britain, France, Germany, Italy, Spain and Portugal combined—the American negotiators swiftly agreed to a price of S15 million. The treaty added 828,000 square miles of land west of the Mississippi River to the United States for roughly 4 cents an acre.

[14] MSNBC, Rachel Maddow Show, October 27, 2010

[15] *Healthy Behaviors: Addressing Chronic Disease at Its Roots.* Grantmakers In Health's Issue Brief No. 19, Fedruary 2004. Grantmakers In Health is a nonprofit, educational organization which helps foundations and corporate giving programs improve the nations health.

*Influence of Individual and Combined Health Behaviors on Total and Cause-Specific Mortality in Men and Women.* Archives of Internal Medicine, Vol. 170 No. 8, April 26, 2010

[16] Bertrand Russell, *Principles of Social Reconstruction,*1916, pages 165-166

# Acknowledgements

*A Poem About Listening.* Reprinted with permission from *Teen Times*, the national magazine of Family, Career and Community Leaders of America, Vol. 35, Number 2

Charlie Rose interview with Tom Friedman, September 9, 2008. Transcript provided courtesy of CHARLIE ROSE, www.charlierose.com

*Get Over Yourself,* April 30, 2001. *FORTUNE Magazine*, author Patricia Sellers, ©2001 Time Inc. All rights reserved.

*How to Win Friends and Influence People* by Dale Carnegie.
Copyright © January 1, 1936. Simon & Schuster.

Taken from *Myth of a Christian Nation* by Gregory A. Boyd.
Copyright © May 1, 2009 by Gregory A. Boyd. Used by permission of Zondervan. www.zondervan.com.

*Stoking Fear of The Other.* With kind permission of author Neil Steinberg, news columnist at the Chicago Sun-Times.

*Wealth Addiction* by Philip Slater. With kind permission of Philip Slater.

Printed in Great Britain
by Amazon